Llangollen Artist

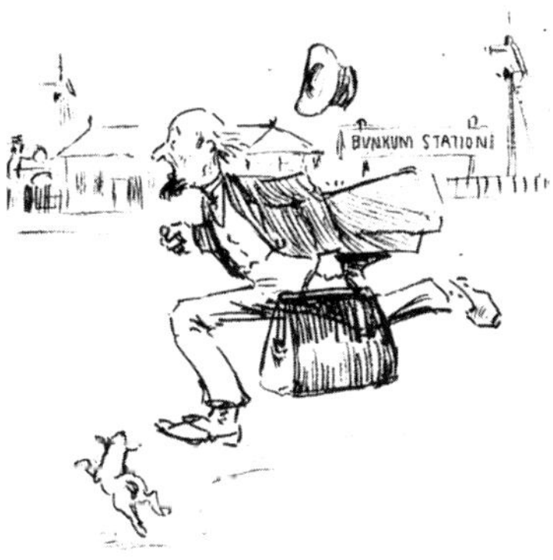

This book is dedicated to the memory
of my father and mother

Sydney Maurice William Burrows
(1917–99)

and

Margaret Ann Burrows
(1922–2008)

Llangollen Artist

– the life, work and postcards of Ernest Burrows

Christopher Burrows

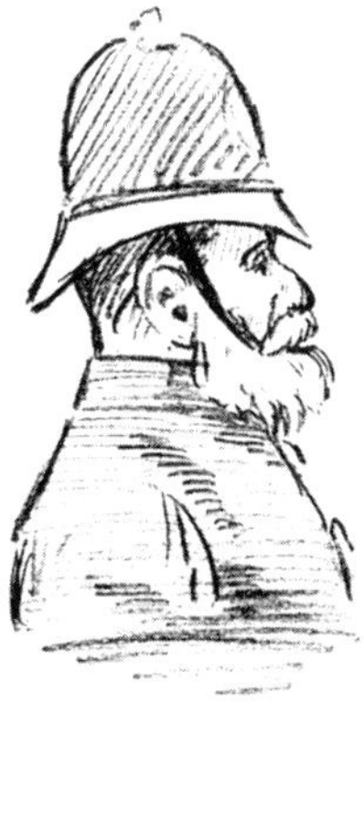

Llangollen Artist
– the Life, Work and Postcards of Ernest Burrows
First published in Wales in 2010 on behalf of the author
by
BRIDGE BOOKS
61 Park Avenue
WREXHAM
LL12 7AW

A CIP entry for this book is available from the British Library

ISBN 978-1-84494-064-6

Printed and bound by
Gutenberg Press Ltd
Malta

Contents

Foreword

As a longstanding collector of Welsh Lady Postcards, it is a privilege to write this foreword.

The work of Ernest Burrows first came to my attention following the purchase from me of a comic postcard by Chris Burrows over the internet. When Chris told me that Ernest was his grandfather, my fascination grew as did my friendship with Chris. This publication is the definitive guide to the work of Ernest Burrows and one should not underestimate the many hours of research which Chris has put into its production. A collector is always grateful and indeed reliant upon an authoritative work to assist them. This publication written and researched by Ernest Burrows' grandson will prove invaluable for all future collectors.

Lynne Peate

Acknowledgements

I would like to thank the following who have assisted in providing invaluable information and postcards from their treasured collections to make the publication of this book possible :

Gordon Owen, Holyhead
The late Eifion Roberts, Conwy
David & Lynne Peate, Llanfair Caereinion
David Rye, Editor, *The Welsh Lady* magazine, Milford Haven
Karlyn Goulborn, Secretary, North Wales Postcard Club
Llangollen Museum and all its staff
Liverpool Museum
Liverpool City Library
National Library of Wales
National Museum of Wales

and last but not least, my thanks to family members for their great help in providing information about family history and pictures.

Christopher Burrows
2010

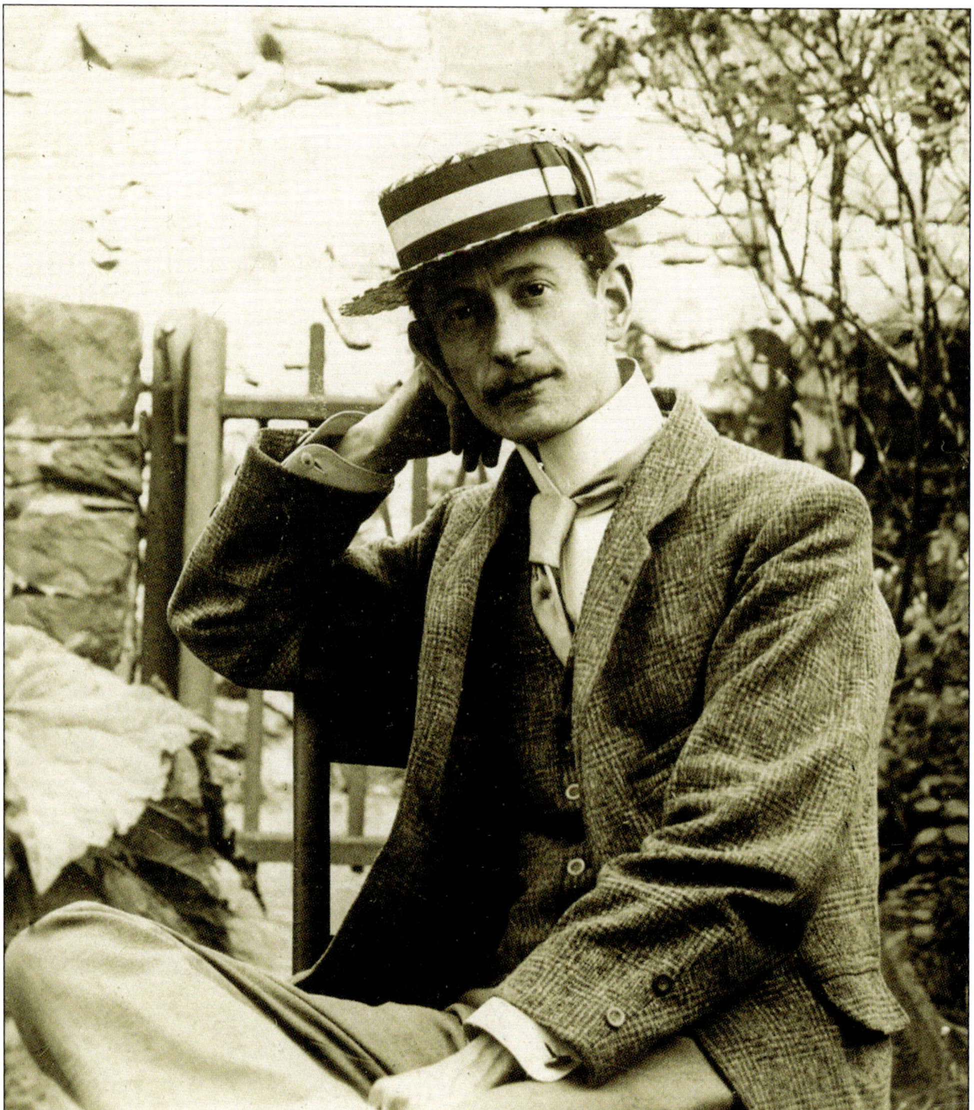

Ernest Burrows

Llangollen in the early 1900s

Llangollen was not a pretty town in the late 1800s, early 1900s. The buildings were dark and glum looking and in the winter months, a cloud of smog hung over the town and this could be seen from the Horseshoe Pass and surrounding mountains. That, however, was the case in many towns in those days – cooking and heating were reliant on coal fires – every building had a chimney!

The population of Llangollen at that time was about 3,000. On most days in the winter months the streets would look quite empty with only the occasional person here and there going about their business. With the coming of the spring and summer, the town would burst into life again with the influx of visitors – the population would double in a matter of weeks.

The reason for this influx of visitors was the setting and beauty of the scenery around Llangollen. With steep green hills to the north and south of the town and entrances to the verdant valley to the east and west, the valley was split into two by the beautiful river Dee, with the ancient fourteenth-century bridge uniting the two parts of the town. People visited in their thousands in the summer months to breathe in the fresh air and to clear their lungs of the smog and dust of the cities.

With the coming of the railway to Llangollen fifty years earlier, people were able to travel from further afield, from the big cities of Manchester, Liverpool,

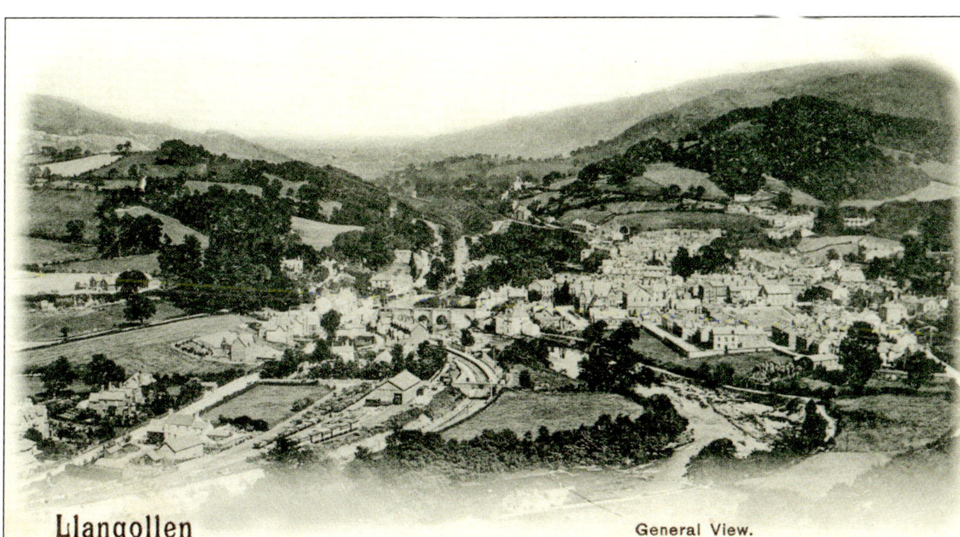

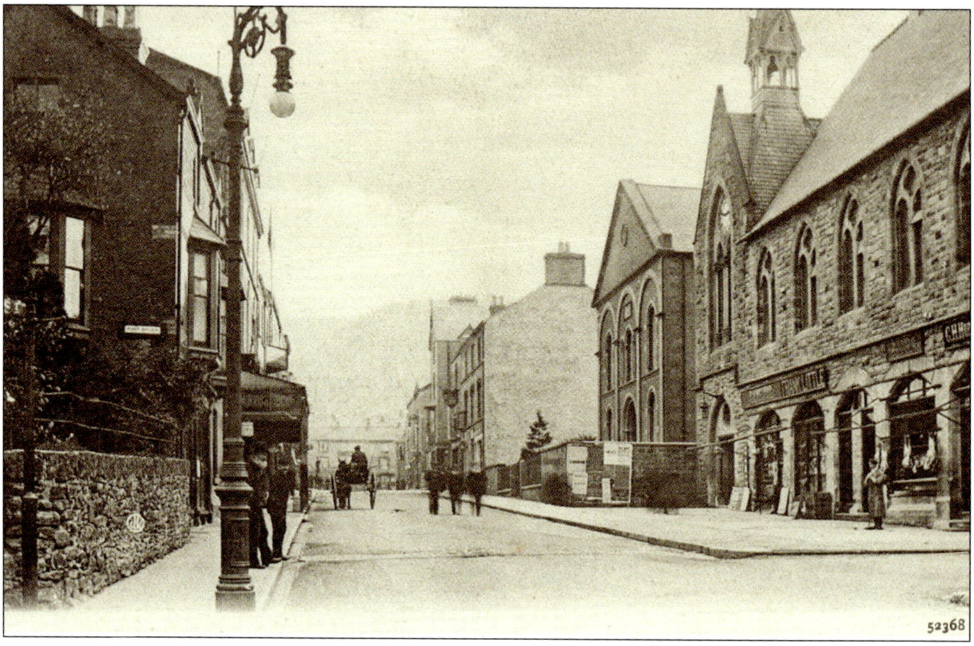

Castle Street, Llangollen.

Birmingham and even London. Weekend travel, and even day trips, became possible as the trains stopped more and more frequently at Llangollen.

The town was totally self-sufficient at this time, having its own woollen and flannel mills, breweries, corn mills, tannery, slate quarries etc. You name it, Llangollen had it! The shops sold absolutely everything one needed and hardly any commodity was worthy of a journey out of town. The butchers had their own slaughter houses, the greengrocers had their own allotments to grow their fruit and vegetables and numerous bakeries baked their own bread and cakes.

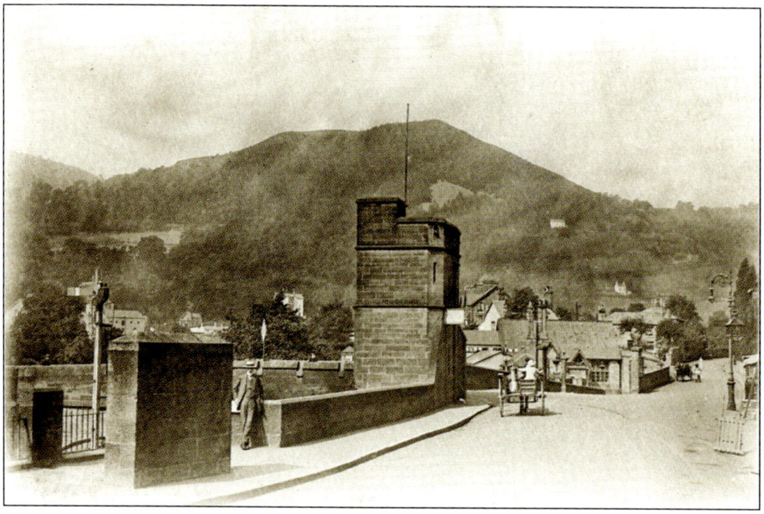

Bridge End, Llangollen.

The only things imported into the town were new fashions in clothing and the odd household item, nearly everything else was produced in the town itself and surrounding area.

Llangollen boasted seven hotels, nineteen inns and so many guest houses and boarding houses that it seemed as if nearly every house in the town took in lodgers during the summer months. It was a great source of income for the townsfolk in the early 1900s.

There was a myriad of places to visit in and around the town. Daily walks to Valley Crucis Abbey, Castell Dinas Bran and along the canal to the Horseshoe Falls. For those who felt less energetic, a trip along the canal by boat was an exciting experience. For others, who were really adventurous, a walk to the top of the Horseshoe Pass was rewarded with views of magnificent scenery. Many chose to follow in the footsteps of the most illustrious characters of the eighteenth century and visited Plas Newydd, the home of the famous 'Ladies of Llangollen'.

The opening of the Victoria Promenade in the 1890s along the riverside proved a popular venue where visitors could sit on the rocks and watch the river Dee flow under the fourteenth-century bridge, one of the 'Seven Wonders of Wales'. The promenade also provided a very romantic

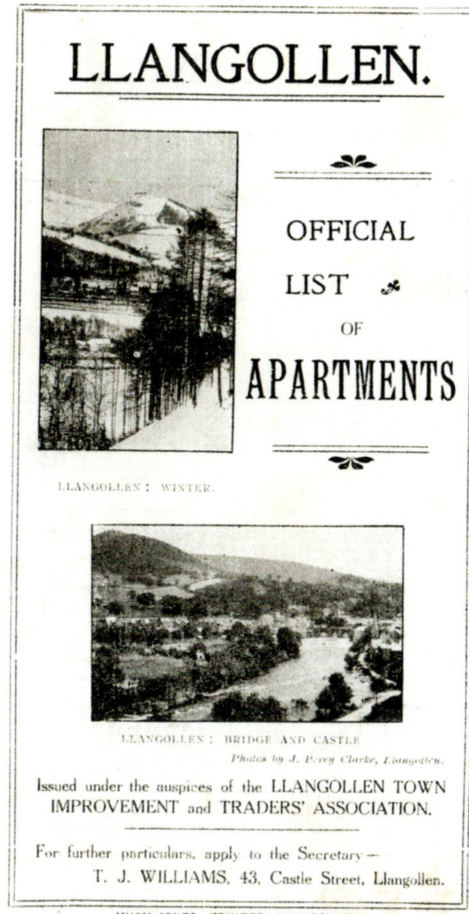
LLANGOLLEN.

OFFICIAL LIST OF APARTMENTS

LLANGOLLEN: WINTER.

LLANGOLLEN: BRIDGE AND CASTLE.

Photos by J. Percy Clarke, Llangollen.

Issued under the auspices of the LLANGOLLEN TOWN IMPROVEMENT and TRADERS' ASSOCIATION.

For further particulars, apply to the Secretary—
T. J. WILLIAMS, 43, Castle Street, Llangollen.

HUGH JONES, PRINTER, LLANGOLLEN.

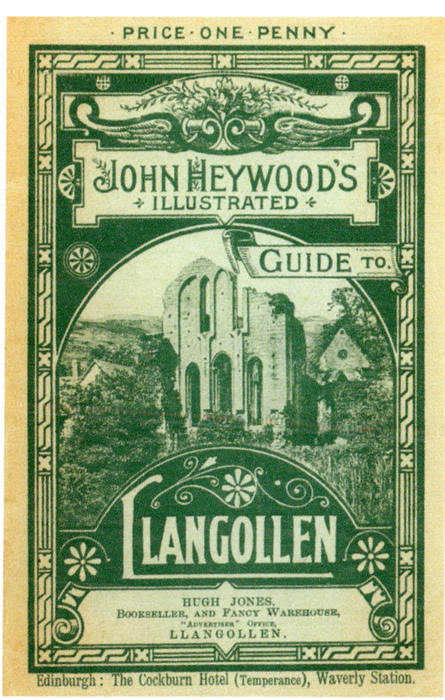

Above: An accommodation guide to Llangollen.

Left: Illustrated tourist guide to Llangollen.

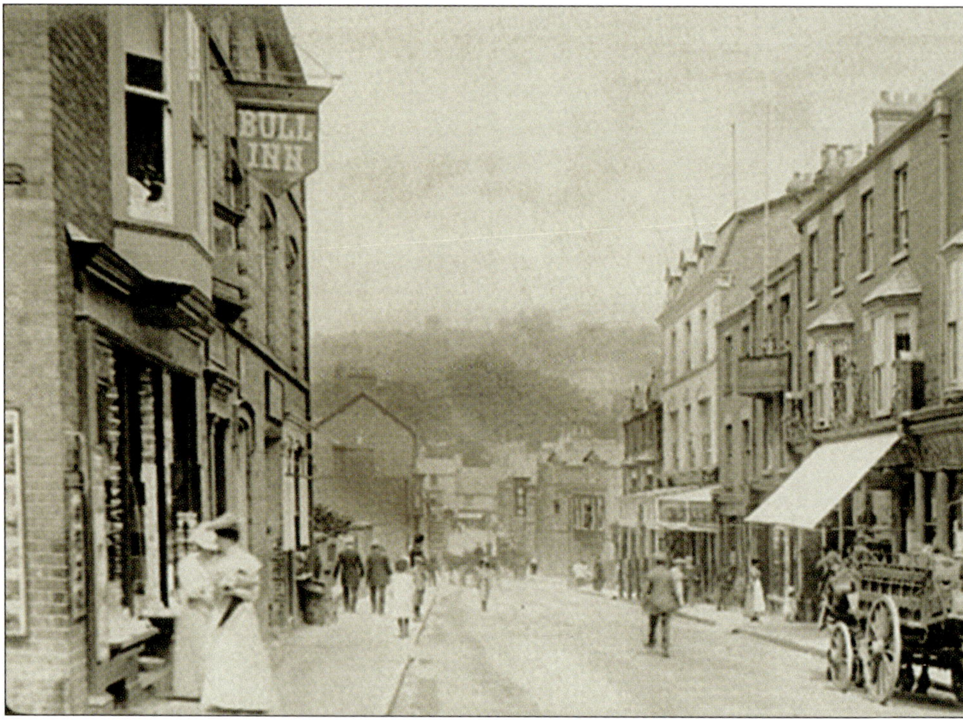

Castle Street, Llangollen, c.1906.

Station approach, Llangollen, early 1900s.

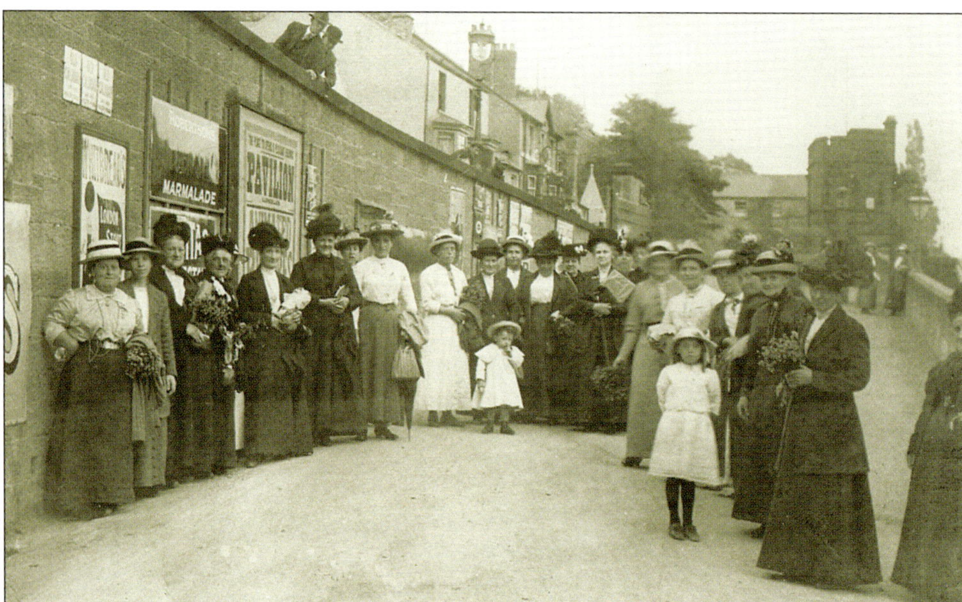

setting for young lovers and newlyweds!

Llangollen was not a place where visitors went hungry as there were many cafés, tea rooms and houses as well as dining halls. It was claimed that the Berwyn Street Pavilion, run by T. M. Rowlands, could accommodate and cater for eight hundred persons and could also provide catering facilities for large picnic parties.

Many of the shops sold postcards of local views, as well as cards which were comical and unusual. Local photographers and entrepreneurs produced their own cards, the earliest of which were by local photographers Lettsome & Sons who had set up a studio in Victoria Square in the last quarter of the nineteenth century. He later had a second shop in Castle Street and the business continued until after the Great War

J. Percy Clarke produced his own

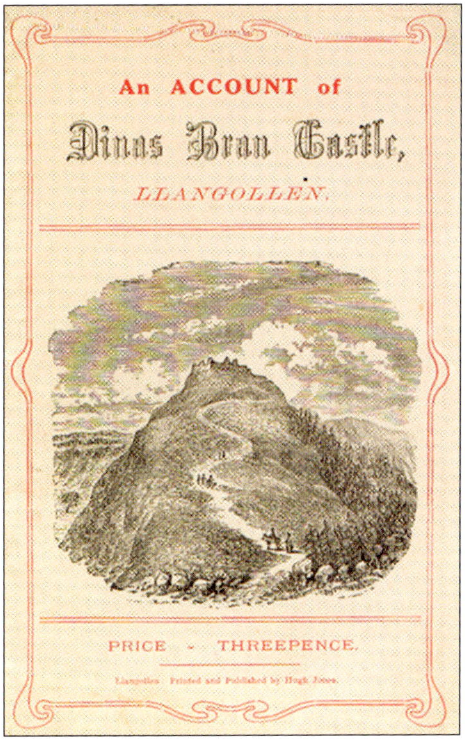
An ACCOUNT of

Dinas Bran Castle,

LLANGOLLEN.

PRICE - THREEPENCE.

Llangollen: Printed and Published by Hugh Jones.

An early guide book to Castell Dinas Bran.

There were plenty of visitors to Dinas Bran in those days.

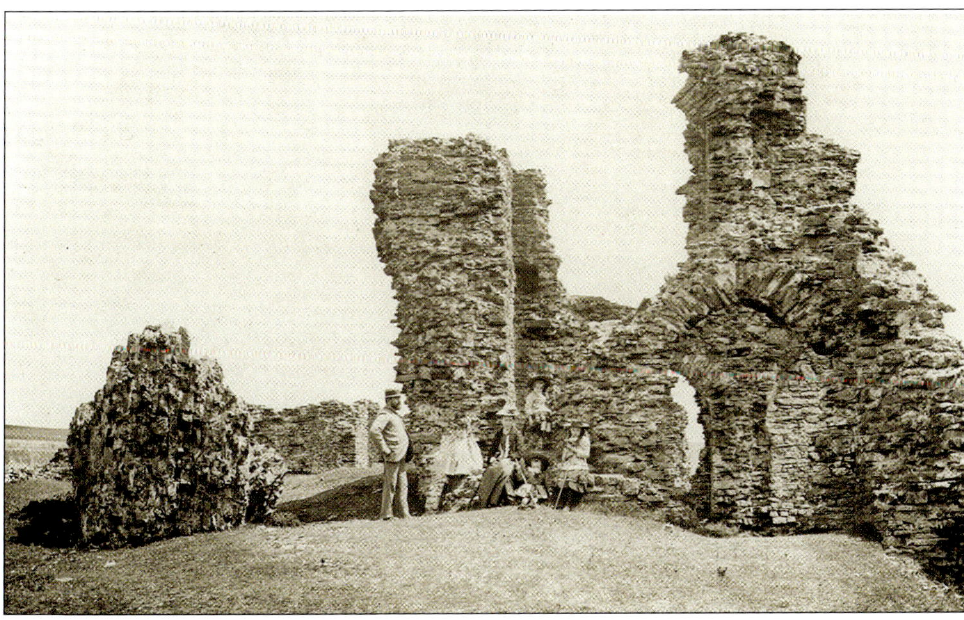

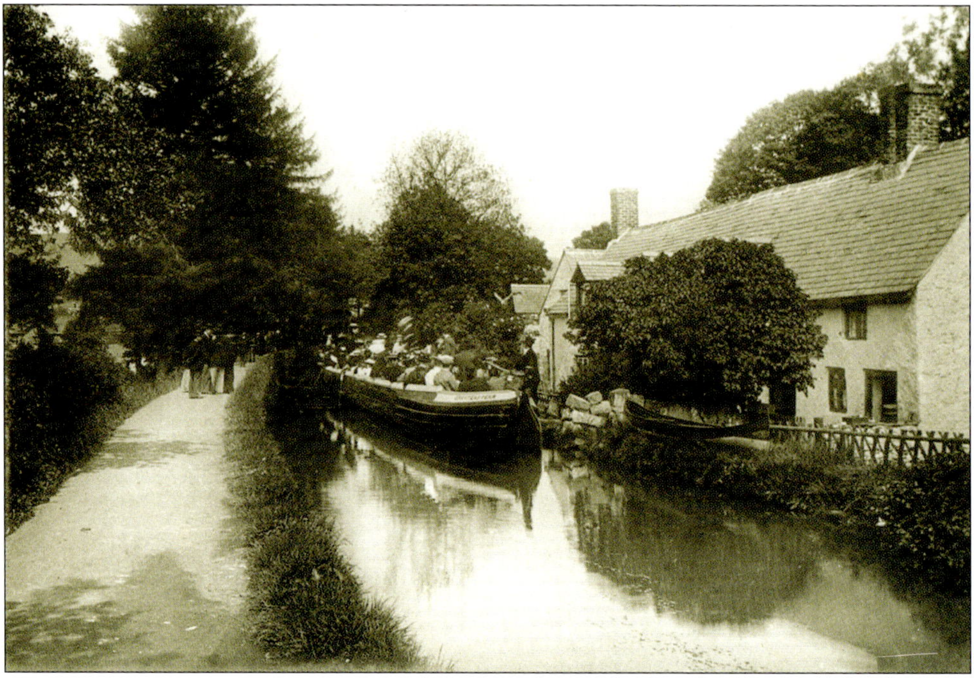

The horse-drawn canal boat Great Eastern *stopping for tea at Penddol Farm.*

Two photographs merged to give one effect.

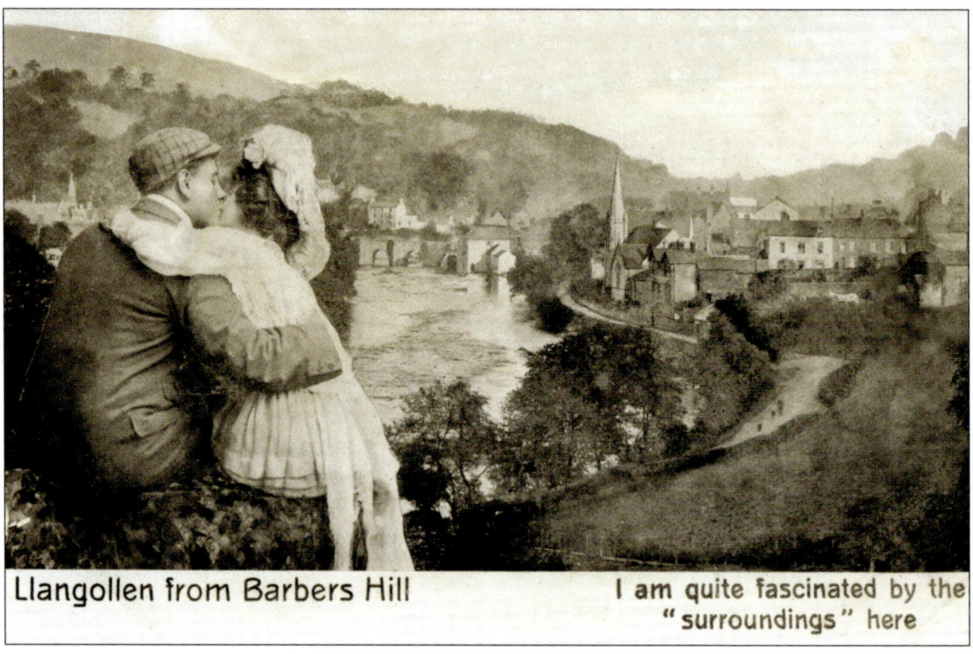

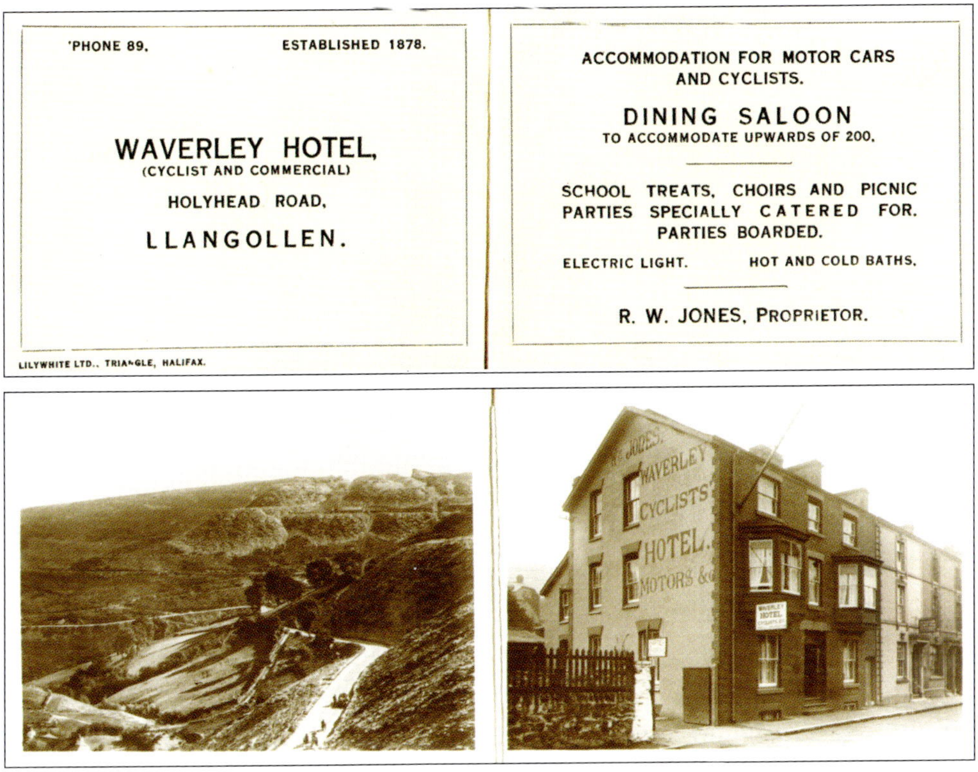

'PHONE 89. ESTABLISHED 1878.

WAVERLEY HOTEL,
(CYCLIST AND COMMERCIAL)
HOLYHEAD ROAD,
LLANGOLLEN.

LILYWHITE LTD., TRIANGLE, HALIFAX.

ACCOMMODATION FOR MOTOR CARS AND CYCLISTS.

DINING SALOON
TO ACCOMMODATE UPWARDS OF 200.

SCHOOL TREATS, CHOIRS AND PICNIC PARTIES SPECIALLY CATERED FOR.
PARTIES BOARDED.

ELECTRIC LIGHT. HOT AND COLD BATHS.

R. W. JONES, PROPRIETOR.

An illustrated brochure for the Waverley Hotel, Holyhead Road, Llangollen, produced in the inter-war period. The photograph on the left shows a view down the Horseshoe Pass.

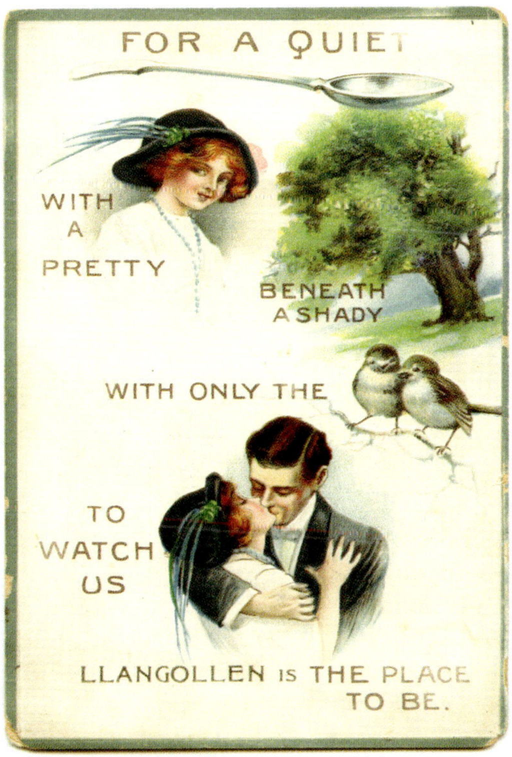

An humorous Edwardian Llangollen postcard.

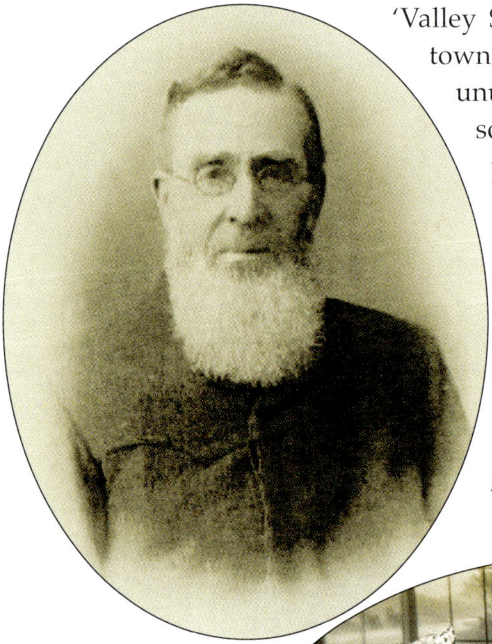

'Valley Series' of cards showing views of the town not usually seen. Some of these had an unusual 'twist' or surprise in that he used some clever early photographic tricks to place unusual objects in the landscape. The following card shows an example of how Clarke superimposed images onto local scenes to create both the possible and the impossible.

So, there we have an illustration of what life was like in and around

Edward Lettsome

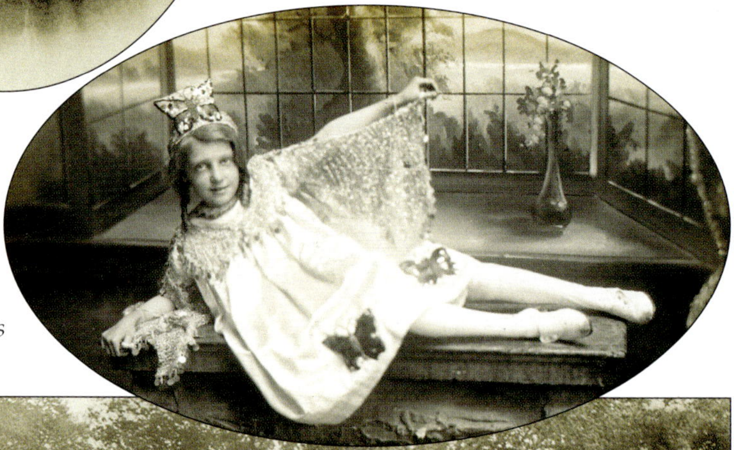

Unknown girl in a fairy costume.

May Queen parade, Plas Newydd, early 1900s.

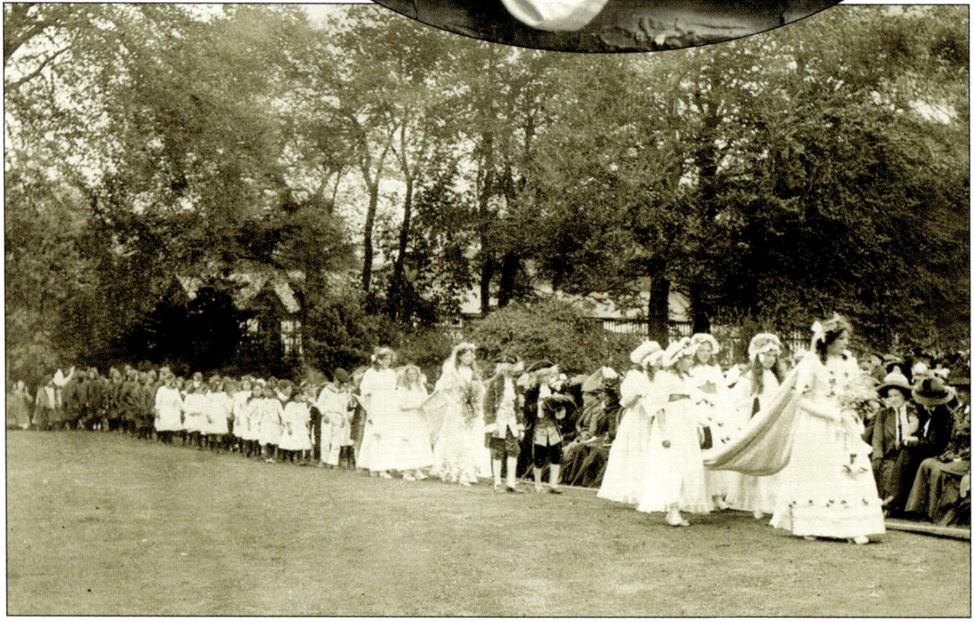

Llangollen at the beginning of the twentieth century when Ernest Burrows was busy painting his pictures and creating his comical Welsh postcards. Llangollen has not changed much over the next 100 years and visitors still come for the same reasons – the only difference being the volume of road traffic and all the problems which that brings.

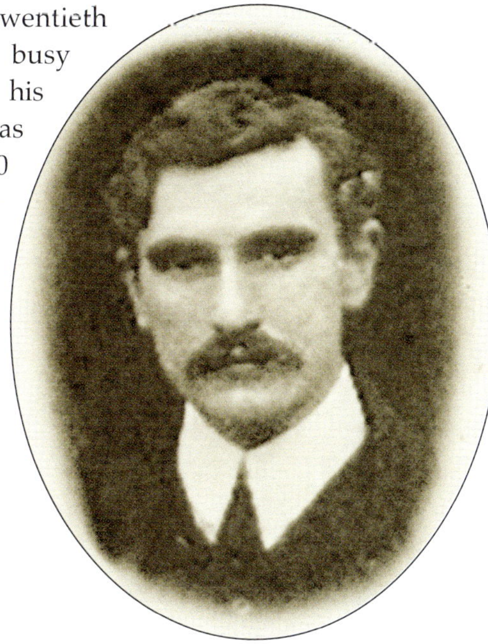

J. Percy Clarke

An example of Percy Clarke's placing of objects in the landscape. The aeroplane has been superimposed over a photograph of the Hand Hotel.

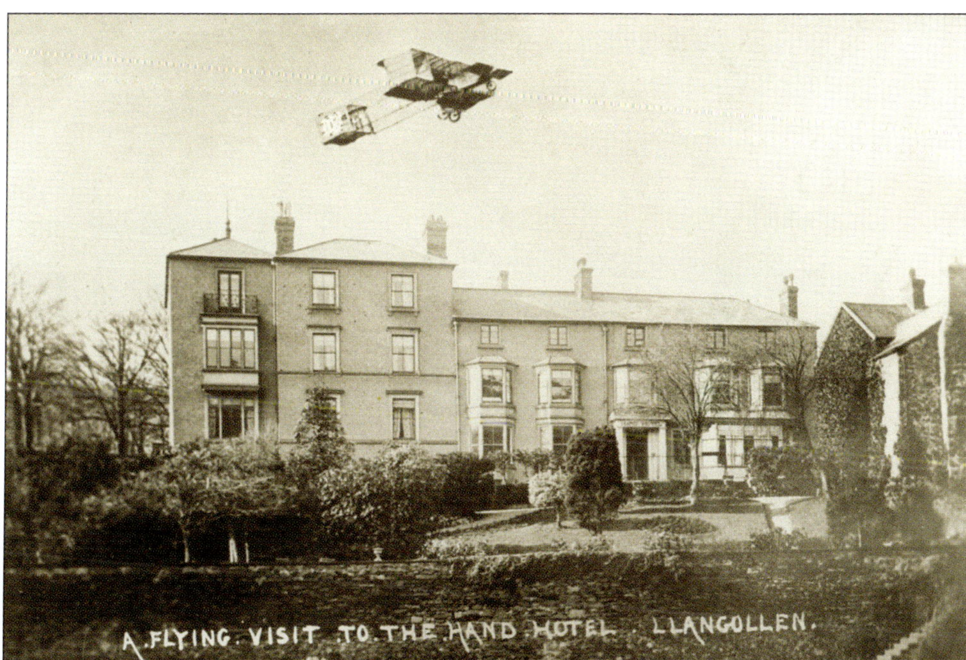

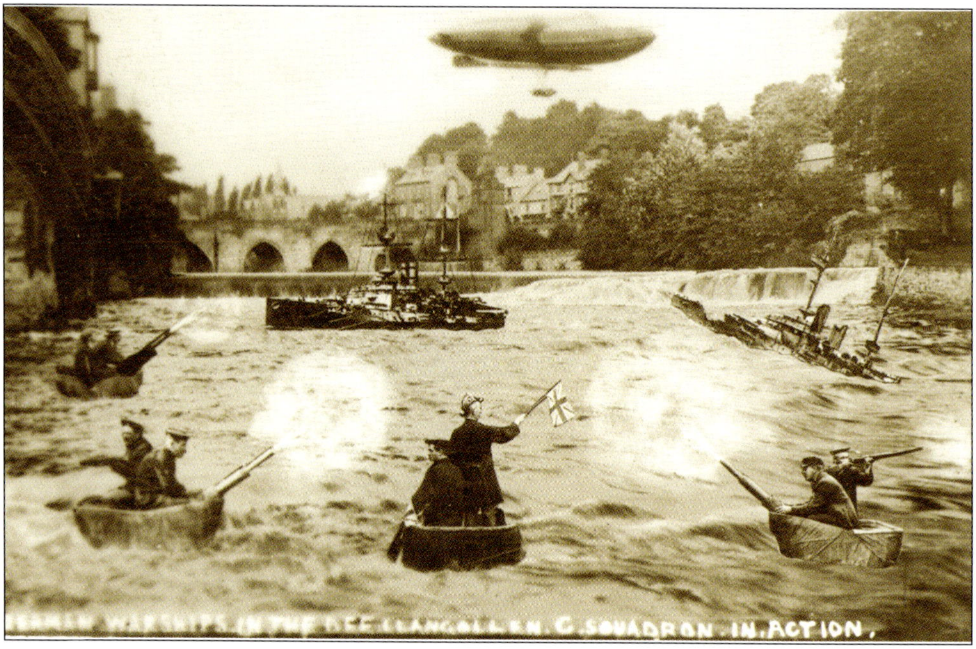

Two examples of taking the 'deciept' one step further, in the above postcard Percy Clarke has locals attacking and sinking German battleships on the river Dee at Llangollen while an airship flys overhead.

Below: A battleship is 'moored' below the bridge in Llangollen.

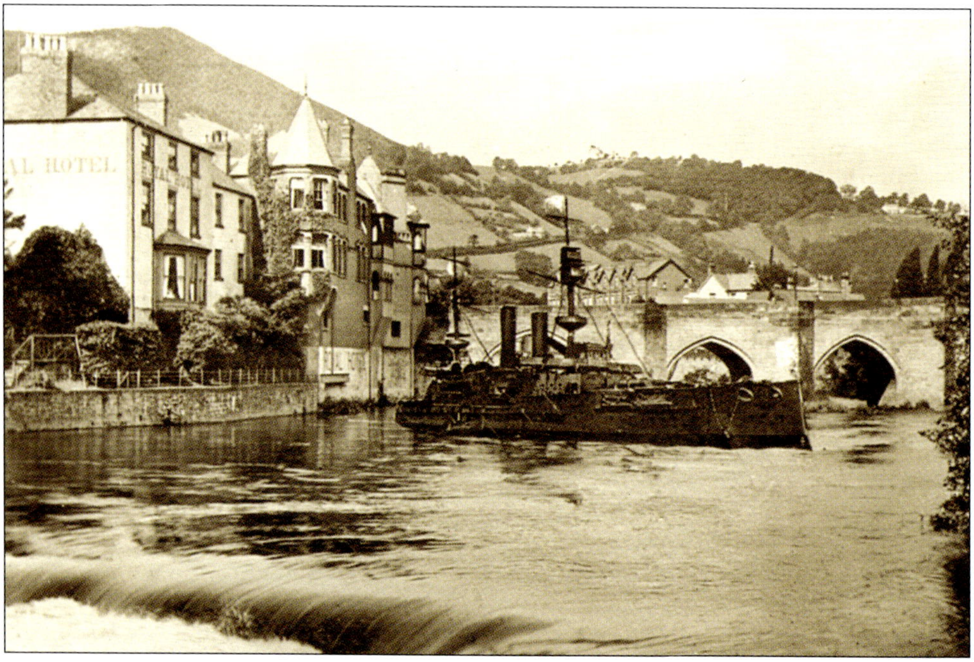

Ernest Burrows
(1869–1918)

Ernest's story begins with his grandfather, Robert Burrows, who was born in Lancashire in 1828 and had built up a well-established butcher's shop in Manchester. In 1846, his son William was born who, when he left school, started work in one of the many cotton mills around Manchester. At that time there were over 560 cotton mills dotted all over Lancashire with over 110,000 workers, some as young as eight-years-old. When William reached the age of nineteen he became a travelling salesman, merchandising cotton goods. The opportunity to escape from the dust and long hours of the cotton mill must have seemed very attractive as the life expectancy of mill workers was very low indeed. William travelled around the country selling his wares wherever he could. His work took him to Wales and eventually to Llangollen where he met a young lady by the name of Mary Jane Roberts. She was the daughter of a well-known local builder, John William Roberts, and his wife Ann. They had two boys and two girls. John, together with his brother Morris, traded locally as M. & J. Roberts & Co, Regent Street, building many fine local buildings including Llangollen Town Hall, the Police Station, the extension on St Collen's Church, the east side row of buildings on Castle Street, an extension on Plas Newydd (now demolished) and the King's Bridge at Berwyn. Other projects included the row of buildings along the seafront in Barmouth and the University Library in Oxford.

Although Mary Jane was four years older than William, they fell in love and a short time later she moved to Manchester. William Burrows gave up his job as a travelling salesman and got a job as a warehouseman in Stockport so that he could be nearer to Mary Jane. They were married in St John's Chapel, Manchester on the 17 October 1867, William was just 21 and Mary Jane 24. They set up home together in Stockport. They returned to Llangollen for the birth of their first child and on the 4 December 1867 Mary Jane gave birth to a baby boy, John. Sadly at five-months-old, John died on 16 April 1868. When they returned to Manchester, they set up home in Chorlton-upon-Medlock where, twelve months later, Mary Jane gave birth to another son, Ernest, on the 21 March 1869. Two years later Ernest had a sister, Lucy, born on 23 Sepember 1871. Another two-and-a-half years passed and another daughter Elizabeth arrived on 6 April, 1874.

The family lived in Manchester for the next four years until William had to give

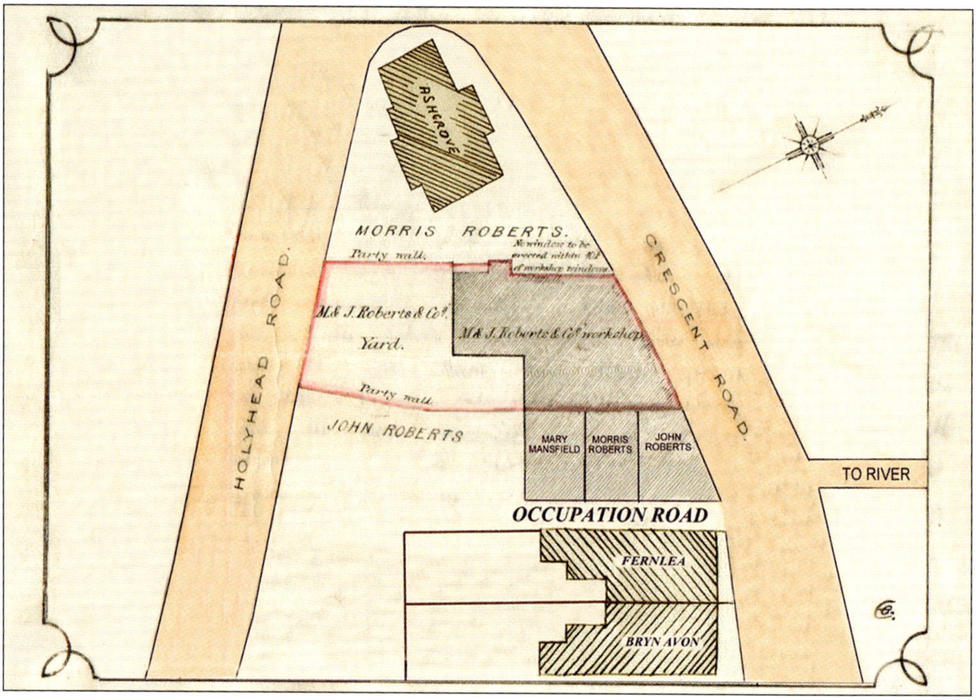

Plan of the land bought and developed by M. & J. Roberts on Crescent Road (now Market Street) Llangollen.

up work due to ill health. There is no doubt that the years working in the cotton mill had taken their toll on him. The family decided to move back to Llangollen to live with Mary Jane's father, John Roberts (now aged 66). By this time Mary Jane's mother had died and, although John had married a woman from Corwen named Sarah Davies, she had only lived for three years after their marriage.

John and his brother Morris had bought a plot of land which was the site of the old builder's workshops in Crescent Road (now known as Market Street) where they built five houses. These are known now as N[os] 1, 2 and 3 Cambrian Place. John lived at N[o] 1, his brother Morris Henry at N[o] 2 and their sister Mary Mansfield (now widowed) at N[o] 3. They also built two houses opposite and known as Fernlea and Bryn Avon (the latter is now known as Croxley). William and Mary Jane moved to live in Fernlea.

Sadly, William's health deteriorated and he died at Fernlea on 13 March 1880 at the age of just 33 years. Mary continued to live at the house, bringing up her young family – Ernest was eleven years old, and his sisters nine and six, when their father died.

With no income, life was hard and Mary started to take in lodgers and before long she had developed a successful boarding-house business taking in lodgers who worked in the town's many shops and businesses. She also took in holidaymakers who would stay for a few days at a time. She did this for many years with several of her guests returning year after year to stay at Fernlea with her and her children.

The two girls, Lucy and Elizabeth eventually moved out, leaving only Mary Jane and Ernest. This meant that there were more rooms, two bedrooms and an attic room (which could accommodate two single beds), for the paying guests. They seemed to manage somehow. Elizabeth became a local schoolmistress and lived with her ageing grandfather, John at Nº 1 Cambrian Place until his death. She remained there until 1925. Mary Jane lived at Fernlea until her death in 1925 aged 83, having bequeathed Fernlea to Elizabeth, who never married and lived there until her death in 1953, aged 79. Elizabeth left Fernlea to her sister Lucy, who moved in with her daughters, Constance and Freda. Lucy died in 1962. Connie and Freda never married and lived at Fernlea for the remainder of their lives. Freda, who worked as a seamstress, died in 1992, aged 81. Connie, who worked behind the counter at the Post Office and served on the Town Council, died in 1994, aged 88.

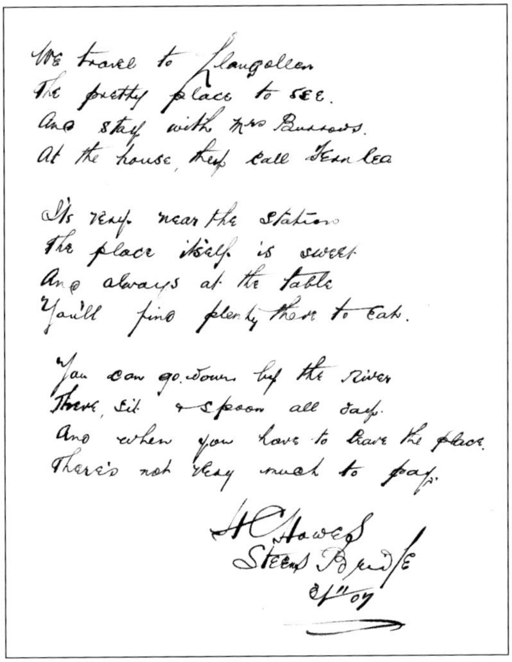
We travel to Llangollen
The pretty place to see.
And stay with Mrs Burrows.
At the house, they call Fern lea

It's very near the Station
The place itself is sweet
And always at the table
You'll find plenty there to eat.

You can go down by the river
There, sit & spoon all day.
And when you have to leave the place
There's not very much to pay.

H C Hawes
Steens Bridge
8/11 07

A poem written by one of Mary Jane's guests, November 1907.

When Ernest left school he became a tinplate worker and eventually a tinsmith. In his spare time he would be found busy with his art and inventions with a particular interest in making working models. In 1885, aged only sixteen, he built a finely-detailed model ship which he fitted into an old drawer. He painted a panoramic background and fitted the ship with a clockwork mechanism. Using an old flour sack which he crumpled up, he placed it beneath the ship and painted it to replicate the sea. When the mechanism was wound up the ship would move up and down on the waves in a rocking motion just like the real thing. The ship still rides the waves perfectly to this day, some 123 years after it was made.

On another occasion, Ernest saw a picture in a magazine of a recording device which had been invented in America. This consisted of a cylinder onto which a wax drum was fitted. A needle, which rested on the drum, picked up vibrations through a horn and engraved them onto the drum. Ernest thought this was marvellous and so, using his skills and ingenuity, set about building his own version. He did so with great success and took it along to the local pub, the

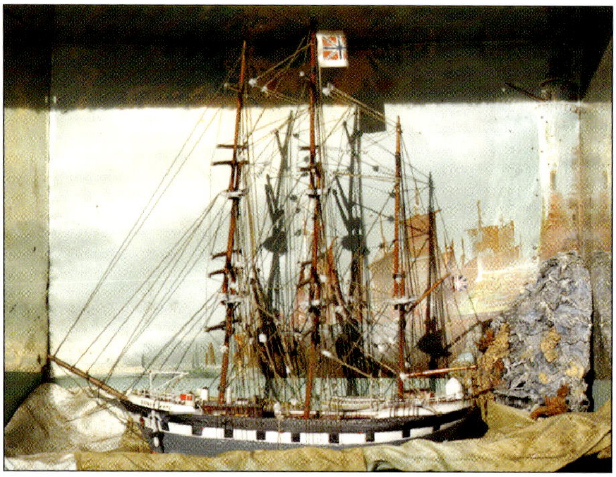

Above: The model ship built by Ernest Burrows, in 1885.

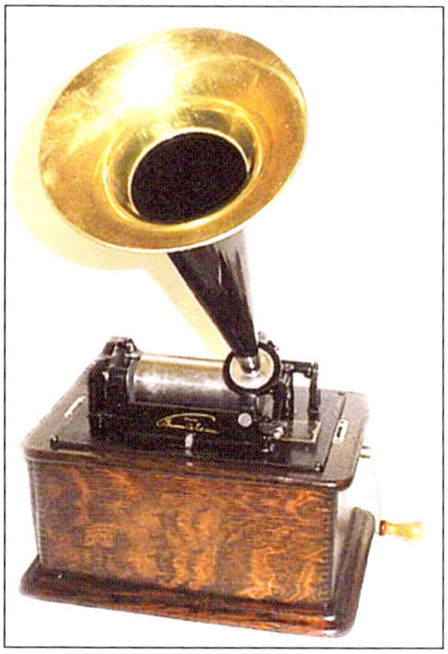

Right: A talking machine similar to that built by Ernest in the early 1900s.

Waterloo Inn (situated at the bottom of Barber's Hill on the Berwyn Road) and set about recording the locals singing Welsh songs. He then proceeded to play back the recording. Everyone in the pub was amazed to hear their own voices singing back to them.

When Ernest was a young man, he was also interested in horseracing. Although not much of a betting man, he appreciated the sport of kings from an artistic perspective. He liked the brightly-coloured silks which the jockeys wore and the beauty of the racehorses, and kept newspaper cuttings of stories about horse-racing life, jockeys, big wins and some of the scams and frauds which were perpetrated. He would carefully paste his cuttings into a big album. One story in the album tells of the best American jockey at the time, one 'Snapper' Garrison. The trainers of his horses were puzzled why there were always slashes in his

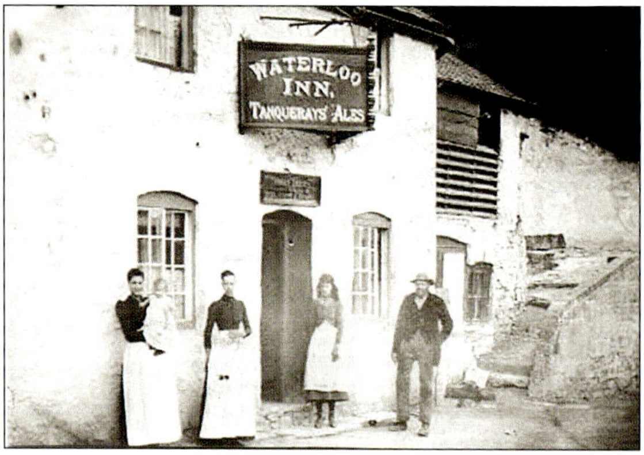

The Waterloo Inn, Llangollen.

saddles after races. It was worked out that Snapper would roll himself into a ball on the finishing straight and the slashes were caused by him jabbing his spurs into the saddle to get more grip!

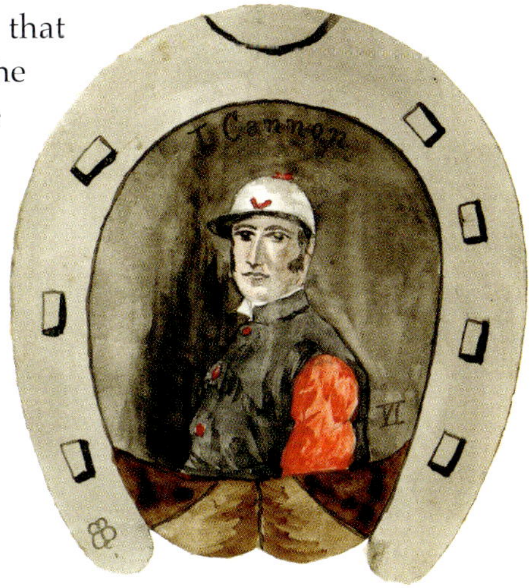

Ernest's painting of 'Snapper' Garrison

Ernest started to draw and paint with great passion. He delighted in sketching local characters and painting the local scenery around Llangollen in oils and watercolours. Eventually his hobby became his profession as, just at that time, the sending of postcards was becoming popular. With his artistic talents and sense of humour, he began to paint comic postcards which he sent to postcard publishers hoping that they would buy them. Thomas Brothers, a printing and publishing business at Everton Road, Liverpool, had an interest in, amongst other things, Welsh comic postcards. They liked Ernest's work and he produced over 100 different paintings for their Everton [Beacon] Series of postcards.

As Ernest grew older, he expanded his field in art, creating many book illustrations, advertising posters as well as undertaking work lettering on railway wagons. His day would often comprise getting up at dawn, walking the six miles to Chirk railway sidings where he would spend the day marking out and painting

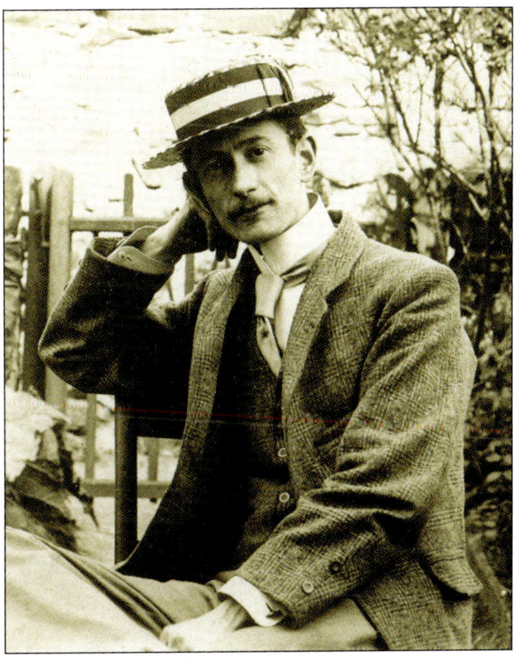

The only surviving photograph of Ernest Burrows.

the lettering on the wagons until the fading light forced him to stop work. He would then walk back to Llangollen in the early evening. After his evening meal, he would work on his postcard paintings until bedtime.

Ernest was a quiet, softly spoken man, always smartly dressed, who with his straw boater would have seemed more at home at Eton or Harrow. He was just under six-feet tall, very slim and sported a small moustache. His face was thin and drawn, but he had smiling friendly eyes and was very approachable in his manner.

He used to spend hours on his own walking around Llangollen and the surrounding countryside, his sketchbook always close to hand. He would sit in the town studying and sketching the locals as they went about their daily chores and chat with the odd one who would stop to look at his drawing and comment on his work. Other times he would be up in the local hills taking in the beauty of the scenery which surrounds Llangollen, away from the hustle and bustle of the town. Sometimes he would take his easel and paints and spend the whole day on the mountainside just painting the scenery.

On cold and rainy days, he would be indoors working on the kitchen table, by a roaring fire, painting in oils or watercolours from the drawings he had made in his sketchbook. Although this may sound like an idyllic lifestyle, times were hard and he had to rely on selling as much of his work as possible. Sometimes he would have to resort to house decorating or sign writing to make ends meet. And there was the cost of his art materials to consider as well as putting food on the table for his growing family.

In his early thirties, Ernest had met a local girl, Melinda Jones from Glynceiriog. In 1904, they married and moved into a small house in Berwyn Street called Rose Place where they lived for many years. Ernest and Melinda had five children: three boys, Wilfred born in 1904; Clifford born in 1906; and Sydney born in 1917, and two girls; Irene born in 1907; and Mary born in 1913.

After his marriage, Ernest continued with his art and illustrating books. He created work for an art magazine in London called *The Studio* and also worked for a large chocolate manufacturer called Velma Chocolate. This company used one of his pictures to advertise their brand of chocolate. The company folded a few years later and there are no longer any records of their products available. It was rumoured within the family that Ernest had been responsible for the creation of the charcters now known as the 'Bisto Kids' as an advert for this company, but the Bisto company firmly refutes this.

With the growing popularity of postcards amongst visitors, Ernest began to include some Welsh words on his comic postcards. Unfortunately, he could not speak Welsh and he had to rely on Melinda's help with translating his copy. That is why some of the Welsh spelling on the cards is slightly peculiar – Ernest wrote them down in the way he thought they should be spelt. The postcards were sold to many Welsh tourist attractions and seaside resorts and proved to be very popular.

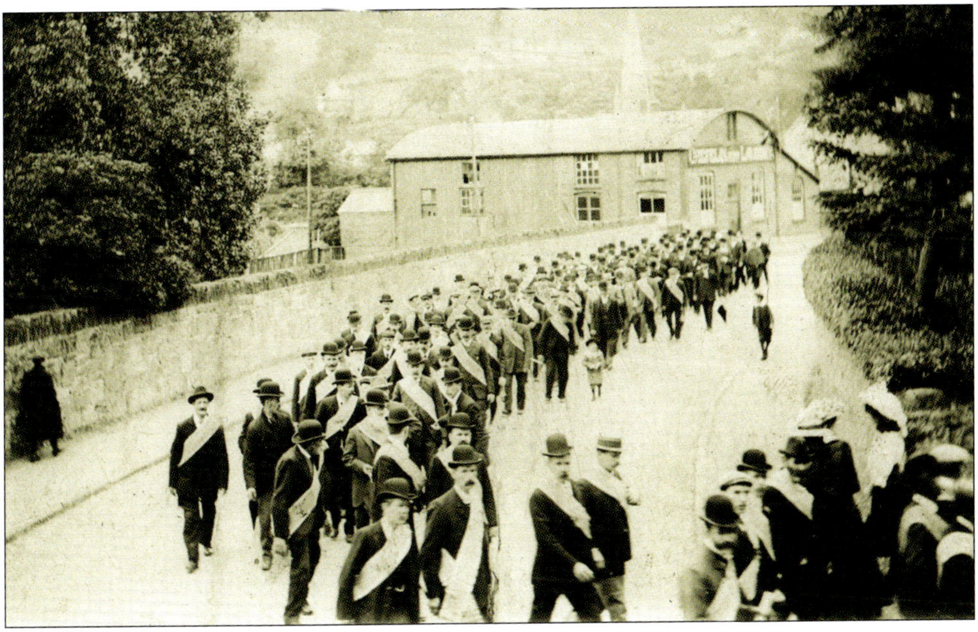

Crescent Road (now Market Street), early 1900s.

Berwyn Street (Rose Place at the top of the road on right), 1900s.

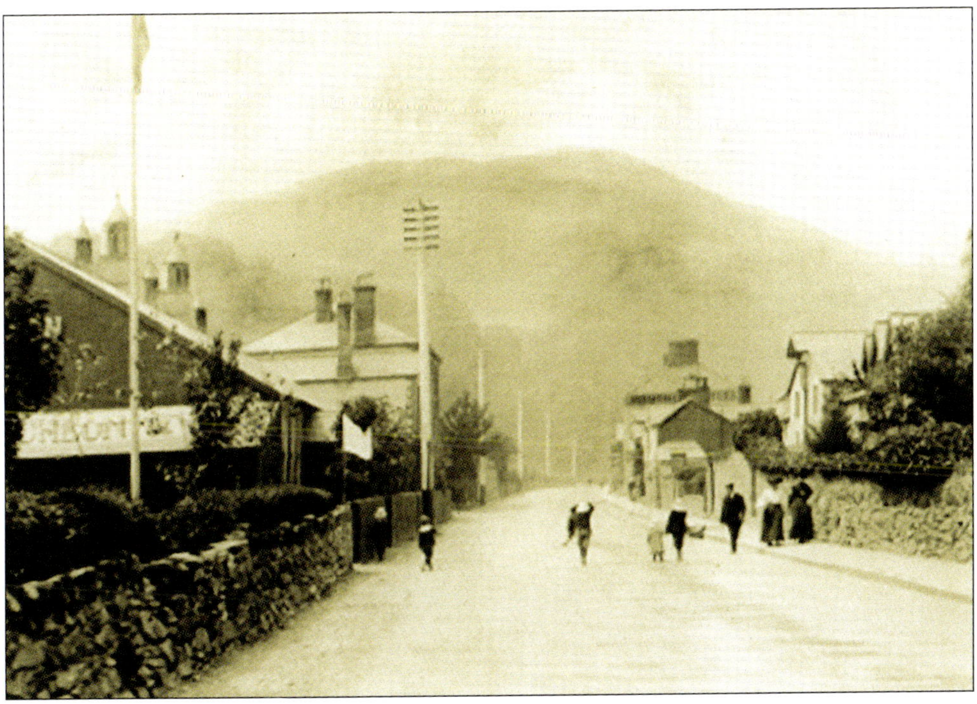

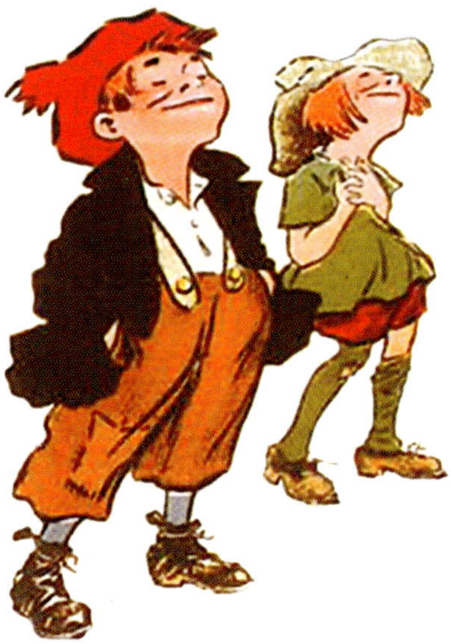

The Bisto Kids.

Sadly, a long and promising career was to be cut short. Soon after the birth of Sydney, his youngest son, Ernest fell ill with influenza. After three weeks of failing health, he died, another victim of the great Spanish-flu epidemic of 1918 which ravaged the country and eventually led to over ten million deaths worldwide.

Ernest was buried in St John's Cemetery on Abbey Road on 14 January 1918. Sadly, his grave is no longer identifiable as, over the years his headstone fell into disrepair and during the Second World War, an airman who was killed when his plane crashed locally was buried on top of Ernest's grave.

Soon after Ernest's death, Melinda and her children moved from Rose Place to a house in Berwyn called Ty Melyn, where they all lived for many years. Melinda continued to live at Ty Melyn with her eldest son, Wilfred, daughter, Mary, and youngest son, Sydney, until she died after a long illness in 1948, aged 67 years.

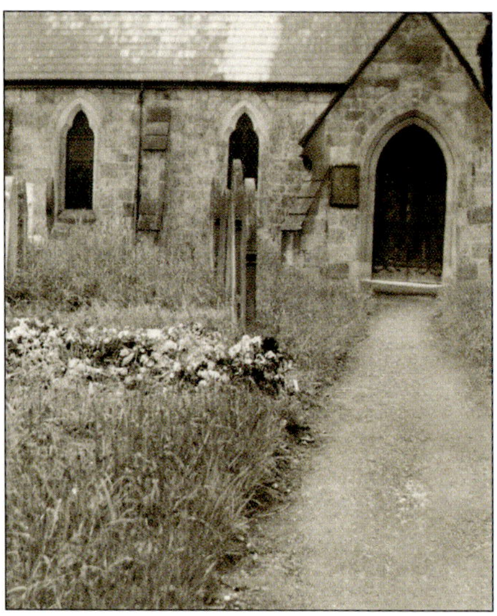

The grave of Ernest Burrows just after the funeral at St John's Church, Llangollen.

The Burrows Family Tree

- Robert Burrows (Born 1828)
  - William = Mary Jane Roberts
    - John — Died 5 months
    - Ernest = Melinda Jones
      - Wilfred = Non Hughes — No children
      - Clifford = Ruth Jones
        - Aurelia = Frank Baxter
      - Irene = Hywel Turner
        - Anne = Ray Bouchier
        - Paul = Katherine Jones
        - Zandrea = Bill Pearce
      - Mary = Sidney Brown — No children
      - Sydney = Margaret Drakeley
        - Christopher
        - Linda = Noel Samuels
    - Lucy = Francis Parry
      - Constance — Unmarried
      - Freda — Unmarried
    - Elizabeth — Unmarried

Ernest's Children

John Wilfred Burrows (1904–63)

Wilfred worked in the forestry during the First World War, after which he became a gardener at Ystrad Hall where he worked for many years for a lady named Mrs Tottenham until she died.

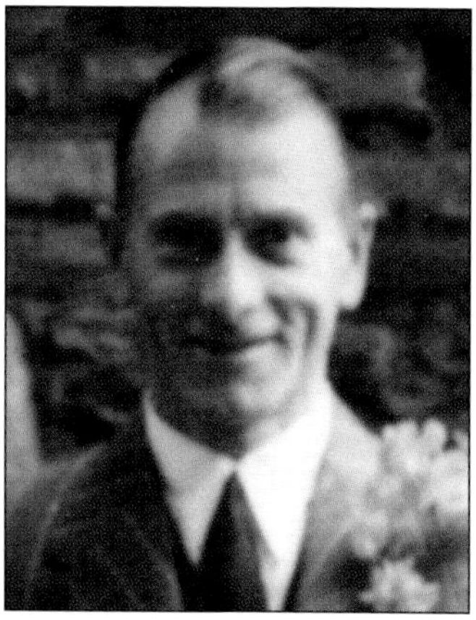

John Wilfred Burrows

At the start of the Second World War he joined the Royal Welch Fusiliers and played in the band which took him to many countries. Wounded in action in 1945, he returned to duty and was posted to Hiroshima after the atomic bomb was dropped. Whilst in Hiroshima he collected many samples of plants and flowers which he pressed and put into a diary along with many photogaphs which he took of the devastation caused by the bomb. The diary is now in the safe keeping of the Imperial War Museum.

After the war, he returned home in 1949 and again took up his gardening, working at the Horticultural Nurseries at Abbey Dingle.

In 1957, He married a girl from Wrexham named Nora Hughes. Wilfred was a close friend of Harry Wheatcroft (the rose expert) and the TV gardener Percy Thrower. He was a regular winner at Shrewsbury, Southport and other great flower shows around the country. Llangollen Flower Show still has a rose bowl trophy named after him. He was also a member of Llangollen Silver Band for many years and would regularly play in concerts and in the bandstand in the park on a Sunday afternoon. He was also a keen darts player and played for the Bull Inn darts team for a number of years. Eventually his months at Hiroshima took their toll and after a long illness, Wilfred died of stomach cancer at his home, aged 59.

Clifford Burrows (1906–64)

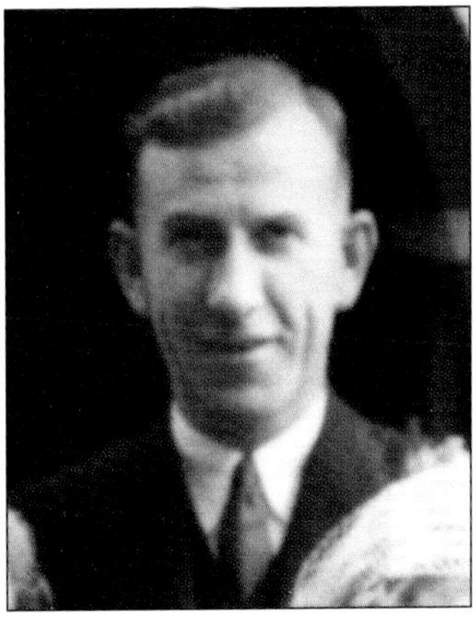

Cliford Burrows

Clifford started work at a bakery in Hall Street Llangollen after leaving school. Eventually he took a job with the Post Office as a telegram delivery boy and later became a postman. After a few years, he met a girl called Ruth Jones from Llanwddyn, a small village on the banks of Lake Fyrnwy. They married in 1934 and had one daughter named Aurelia.

At the start of the Second World War he enlisted in the Royal Welch Fusiliers and was stationed at Colwyn Bay for a short time, before joining the front line. Later on in the war he was transferred to the Royal West Kents. After returning to Britain he was based in Kent until the end of the war. On returning to Llangollen he went back to the Post Office as a postman and after many years service became Head Postman at the Llangollen office,

In his spare time Clifford was a keen cabinet maker and would spend many hours designing and making some lovely furniture – bookcases, cupboards, tables, chairs and stools, all of which were finished to a high standard in his workshop which was located next to his home at the Geraint (the row of cottages just along from Plas Geraint). He lived there for 30 years with his wife Ruth. The house had a wonderful view overlooking Llangollen. He sadly passed away due to a heart attack at the age of 58.

Margaret Irene Burrows (1907–72)

Rene as she was known locally by friends and family, left school in about 1922 at the age of 15. She started work as an assistant at a local shop and worked there for a number of years. Just before the outbreak of the Second World War she married Hywel Turner, a local man who worked for the Bryn Melyn Motor Company in Regent Street Llangollen. Hywel was a keen amateur photographer and eventually started work with the BBC as a sound recordist. They set up home in Llangollen, and just after the war started Hywel was

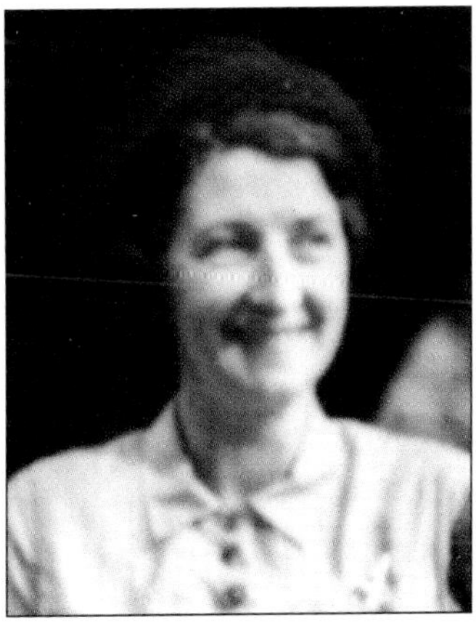

Margaret Irene Burrows

posted to the BBC in Evesham. Later he transferred to Bangor, and finally Cardiff where he worked for many years. Rene worked in the forestry during the Second World War and they had three children Ann, Paul and Zandrea. Eventually Hywel's work took the family to live in Cardiff. After a few years Hywel left the BBC and the family then moved to Fishguard where they opened a radio and TV shop selling television sets, records and other electrical equipment. Later they opened another shop in Haverfordwest. Hywel and Rene ran the shops together for many years until they retired in 1969. The running of the shops was then taken over by their son Paul. Rene was one of the nicest and most generous persons you could ever wish to meet. Sadly, she died after a short illness due to a brain haemorrhage aged 65 and was buried in St John's Cemetery, Llangollen, where the rest of the Burrows family are buried.

Mary Burrows (1913–56)

Mary went to work in Anglesey after leaving school, at the age of fourteen. She started work in service in a large house on the island and was there for a number of years. She then moved back home to Llangollen and worked in the Mile End factory until the outbreak of the Second World War, when she left to join the Women's Land Army, working in the forestry as a Lumber Jill. After the war she went back to Mile End to work as it was near to the family home at Ty Melyn in Berwyn. Eighteen months later her mother, Melinda, suffered a stroke and Mary had to give up work to care for her. For two years she did everything for her mother and looked after the family home with her two brothers Wilfred and Sydney who were still living there until Melinda died in 1948.

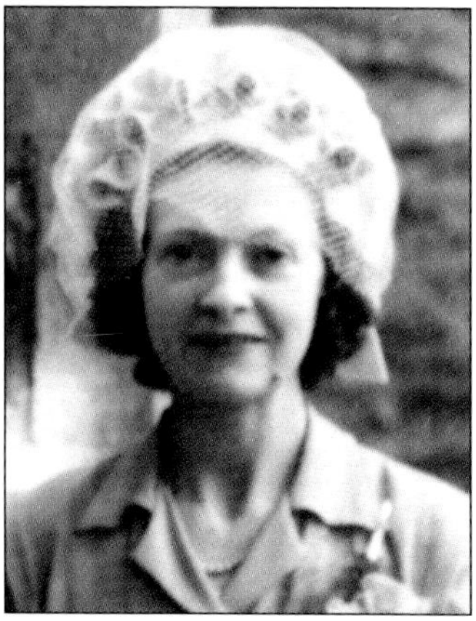

Mary Burrows

Mary was always a very smartly-dressed woman wearing all the latest fashions but she was down to earth and a very homely person.

She started going out with a smartly-dressed local man named Sidney Brown, and in 1951 she and Sidney got married. They moved to the Wrexham area where they both worked in service on a farm in Marchwiel for a couple of years until Mary was taken ill with cancer in 1955, when they moved back to Llangollen to be nearer the family, Sadly Mary lost her battle with the disease and died in 1956 after a long illness at Llangollen Cottage Hospital aged 43.

Sydney Maurice William Burrows (1917–99)

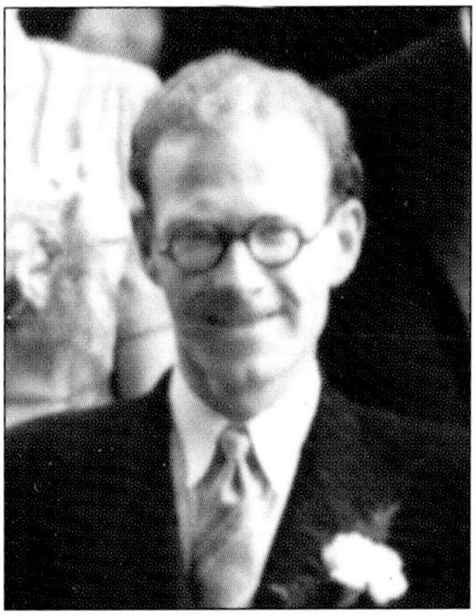

Sydney Burrows

Syd, as he was known locally was a keen cyclist as a young man and would cycle for miles with a club from Wrexham called the Wrexham Wheelers. He started work as a painter and decorator when he left school and served his apprenticeship in decorating and signwriting. In those days signwriting was a large part of the work as most businesses, such as solicitors, banks and public houses, had their names painted back to front in gold leaf on their windows. Syd had a natural talent for this, no doubt passed down from his father Ernest,

At the start of the Second World War, at the age of 22, Syd joined up and was in the Normandy landings, something he would never talk about – no doubt it was too horrific to recall. After the war, he returned to his decorating job and in 1949 married Margaret Drakeley. They eventually went to live at Cambrian Place a house which his great-grandfather had built. Syd and Margaret had two children, Christopher and Linda. Eventually Syd started work at Abbey Dingle Nurseries as a painter and signwriter, working on the many buildings which belonged to the company including the factory belonging to Cuthberts, Dobies and Carters Seeds in the town. Syd also had a great interest in nature and kept reptiles for a time, then tropical birds and eventually tropical fish in which he was a specialist breeder for many years. Syd eventually died of heart failure at the age of 82.

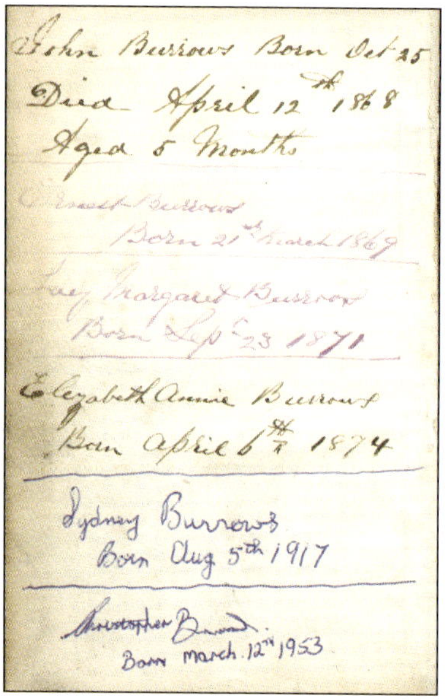

John Burrows Born Oct 25
Died April 12th 1868
Aged 5 Months

Ernest Burrows
Born 21st March 1869

Lucy Margaret Burrows
Born Sep 23 1871

Elizabeth Annie Burrows
Born April 6th 1874

Sydney Burrows
Born Aug 5th 1917

Christopher
Born March 12th 1953

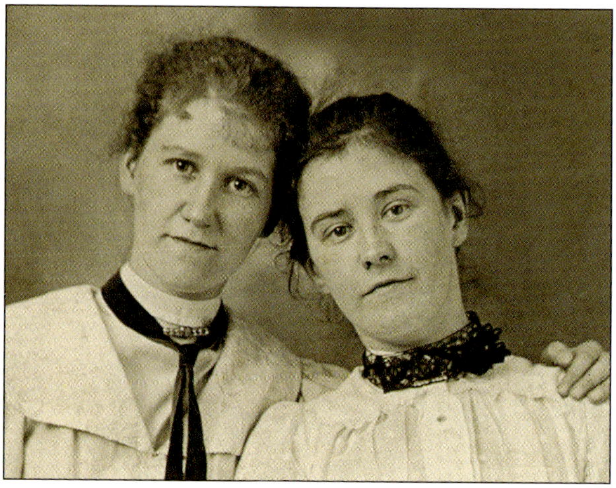

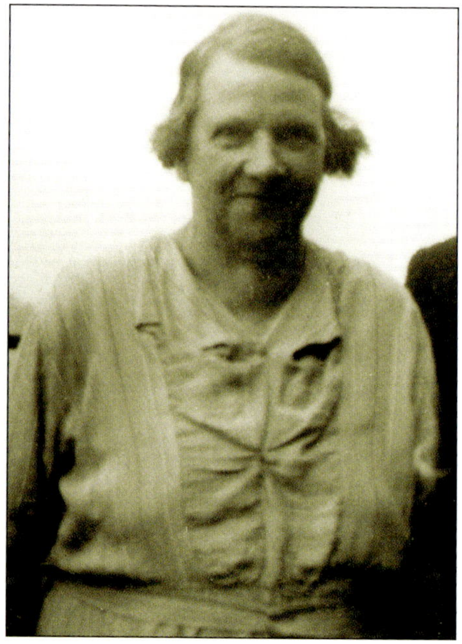

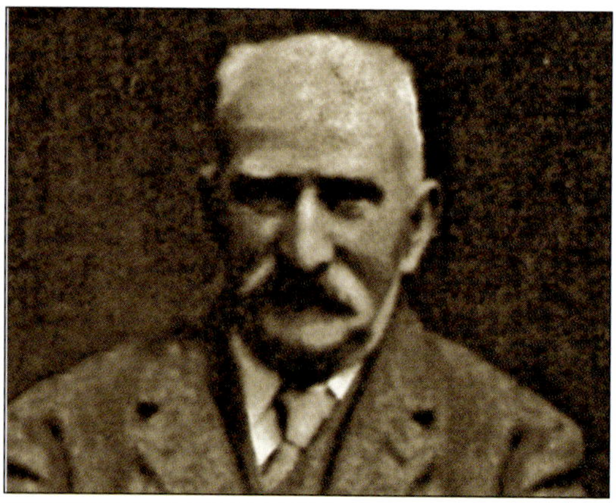

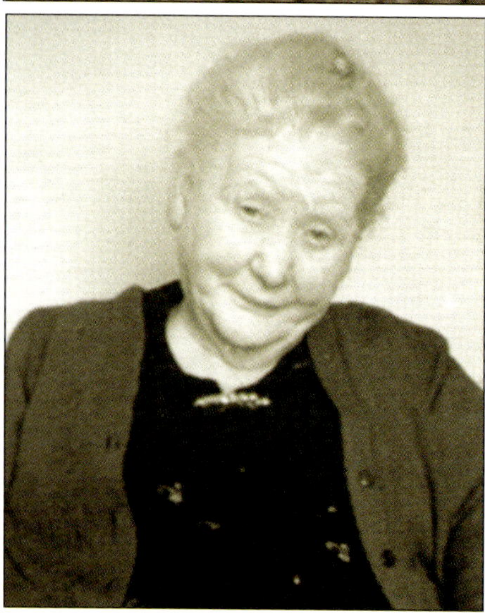

Clockwise, from top left:

A page from the Family Bible given to William Burrows in 1856 by St Mark's Sunday School, Manchester, when he was aged ten.

Elizabeth and Lucy Burrows.

Melinda Burrows.

Lucy Burrows.

Llangollen builder John William Roberts (Mary Jane's father).

The

Ernest Burrows

Postcard Collection

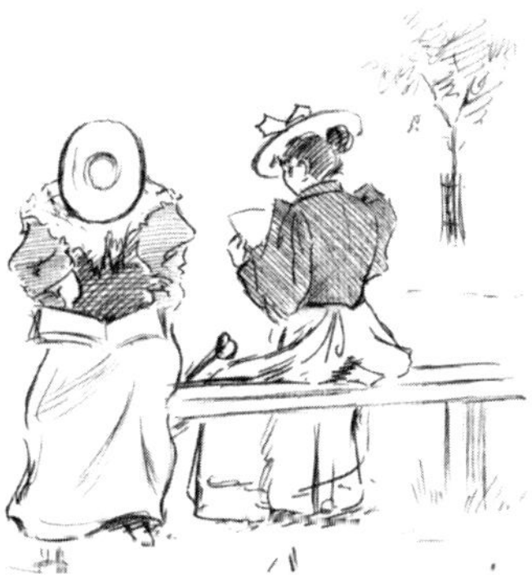

The Everton Postcard Series

The Thomas Brothers and Company are listed in the *Liverpool Directory of Business* as follows:

1895–8	Thomas Brothers, Printers, Stationers and Lithographers, 37 Everton Road, Liverpool.
1901	34 & 37 Everton Road, Liverpool.
1904–07	34, 36 & 37 Everton Road, Liverpool.
1911	34 & 36 Everton Road, Liverpool.

After 1911 no listings appear in the directory. It is said by some that the buildings burnt down in 1922 with none of the records surviving the fire.

The following is an extract from the book *Picture Postcards and Their Publishers* by Anthony Byatt, published in 1978 by Golden Age Postcards.

> Thomas Brothers and Company commenced in business as printers, stationers and lithographers about 1894 at 37, Everton Road, Liverpool and they are still in business today as printers. They say they have no records of their postcards. The trade mark shows a picture of the Everton Beacon Tower which was erected during the time of Elizabeth I to warn of invasion and apparently collapsed in 1803.
>
> The principal purpose of the company was directed to publishing Welsh postcards and these are all entitled *Llythyr Gerdyn* [Postcard]. There are some cards showing Welsh life and costume, but the majority are comic cards which exploit every possible angle of Welsh humour, naturally with particular emphasis on the long and awkward names that the stranger to the principality is likely to find. Early motorists, cyclists and walkers meet at crossroads and scratch their heads at signposts with fingerboards five feet long, or stare at village names running the entire length of the card. The Jones family treks along a country road represented by all its generations with the comment 'Wales was Wales before England wass wass'. Some include verses of rhyme, turning such well-known opening lines such as 'Where are you going my Pretty Maid?' into tongue twisting Welsh teasers.
>
> Many of the Everton Series cards were printed in Germany and numbers extended beyond 3000, although there may be considerable intervals between and many of the earlier cards up to 1905 do not carry a number at all. Cards appear to have been published at least into the early 1920s.

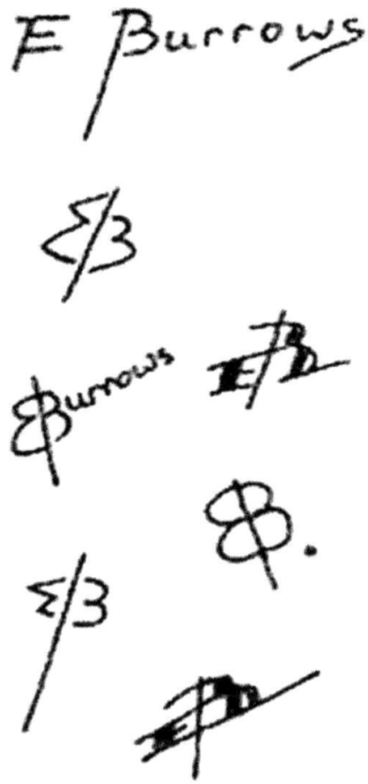

Examples of Ernest Burrows' signatures

The Ernest Burrows postcards which appear on the following pages are all from the Everton Series. Most of the postcards carry an Everton number on the back – either down the left hand side or under the Beacon crest in the centre of the card. However, some cards do not bear a number at all either because the cards were not sent to Thomas Brothers by Ernest or because they were released before numbering commenced. The cards featured here show the relevant Everton number under each card. They appear in no particular order and it is unlikely that the collection is complete as from time to time an unknown card by Ernest comes to light! Although some cards may look the same, they may carry different numbers possibly because the cards were reissued at some later date.

It will be noted that not all Ernest's cards are signed by him. Those which are signed carry a variety of signatures, others are just initialled. Some cards carry no identification and it is thought that these may have had the signature or initials removed by Thomas Brothers and were issued after his death. They were removed possibly in avoidance of royalties which would have been due to the family.

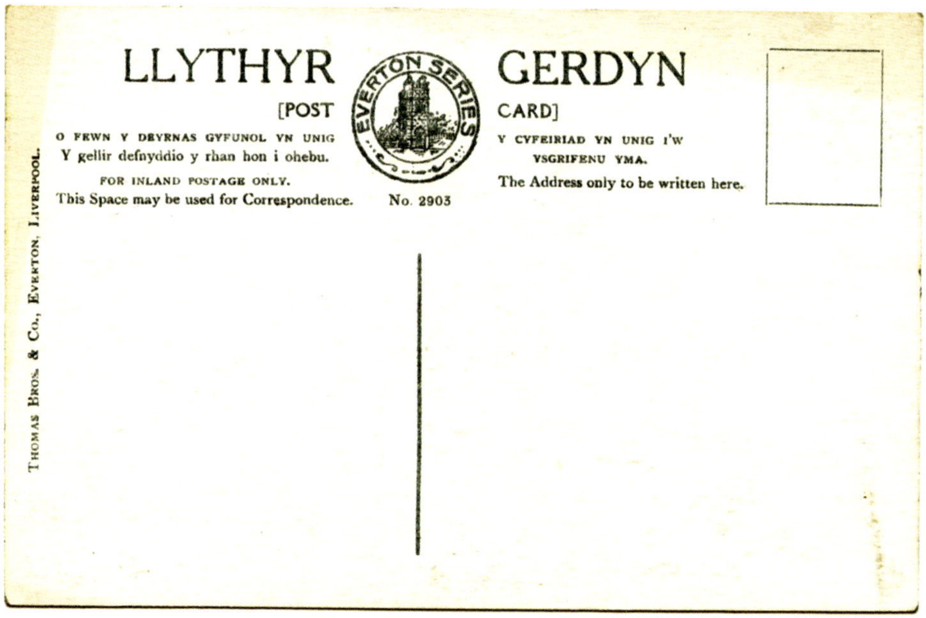

Two different types of Everton postcards. One written in bilingually with Welsh first; the other in English only. Note the bottom card printed in Saxony, Germany.

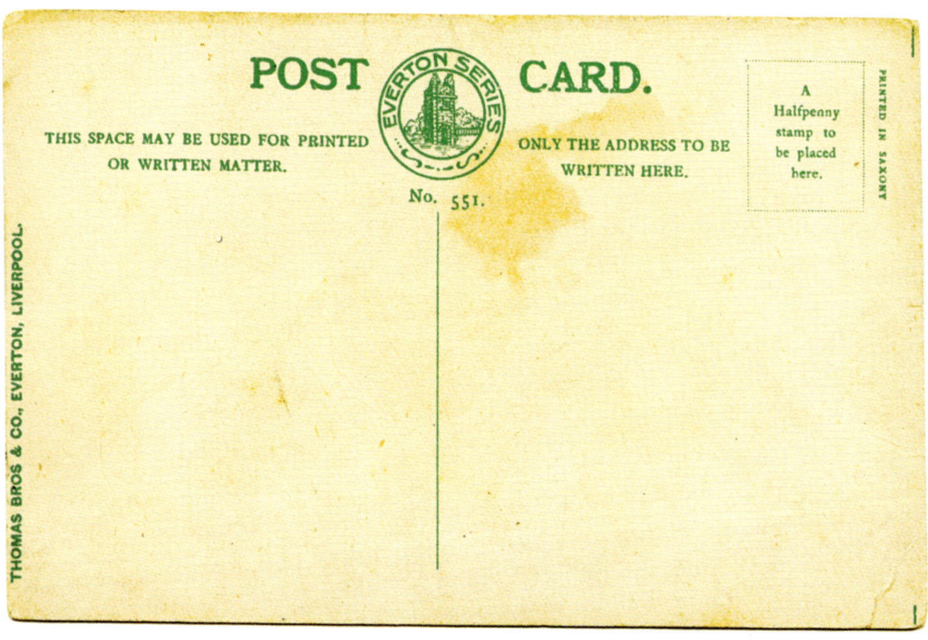

Ernest Burrows Postcards

Thomas Brothers Everton Series
Numbers recieved so far
All postcards published between 1900 and 1922

201
202
203
204
205
206
207
208

215
216

218

226
227

229
230
231
232
233

235
236
237
238
239
240
241
409

411
412
413
414
415
416
417
418

420

422
423
424
425

453
455
456

458

522
523

526
527

550
551

606

1001

1009

2404

2407

2410

2513

2600

2604

2903

3003

3008

3109

3604

3803

3901

3911

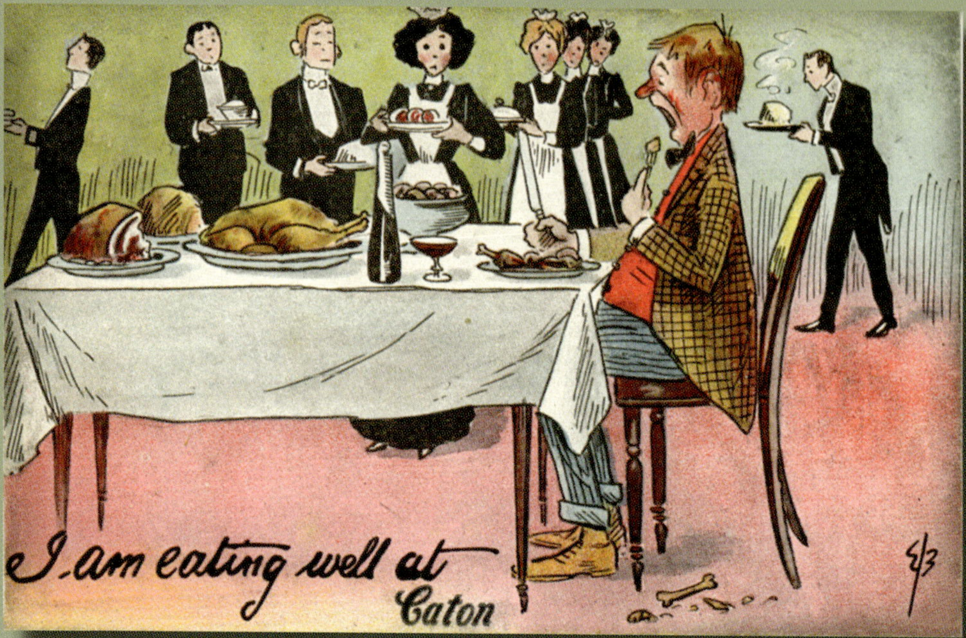

No. 416

No. 3901

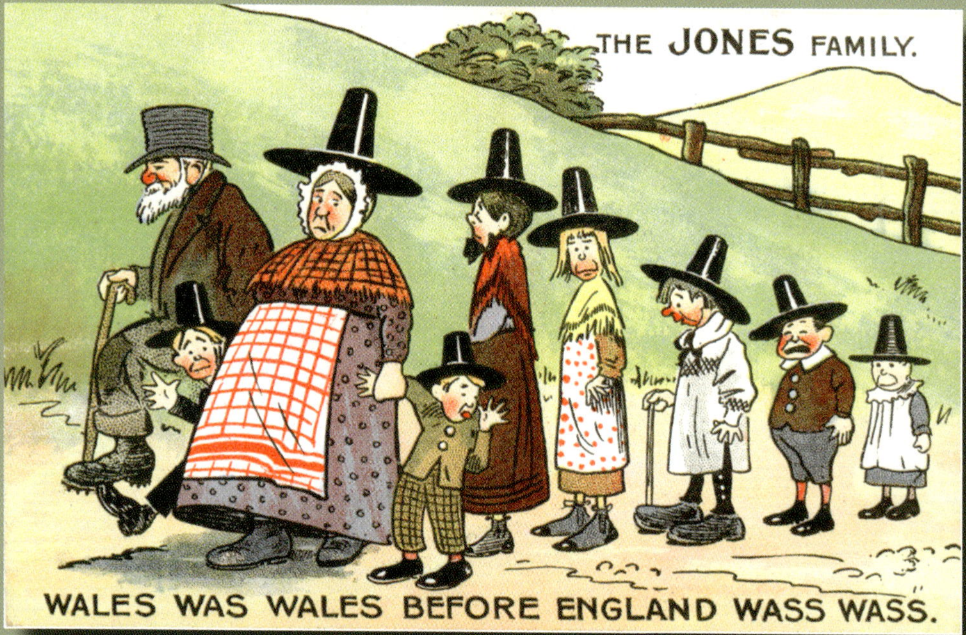

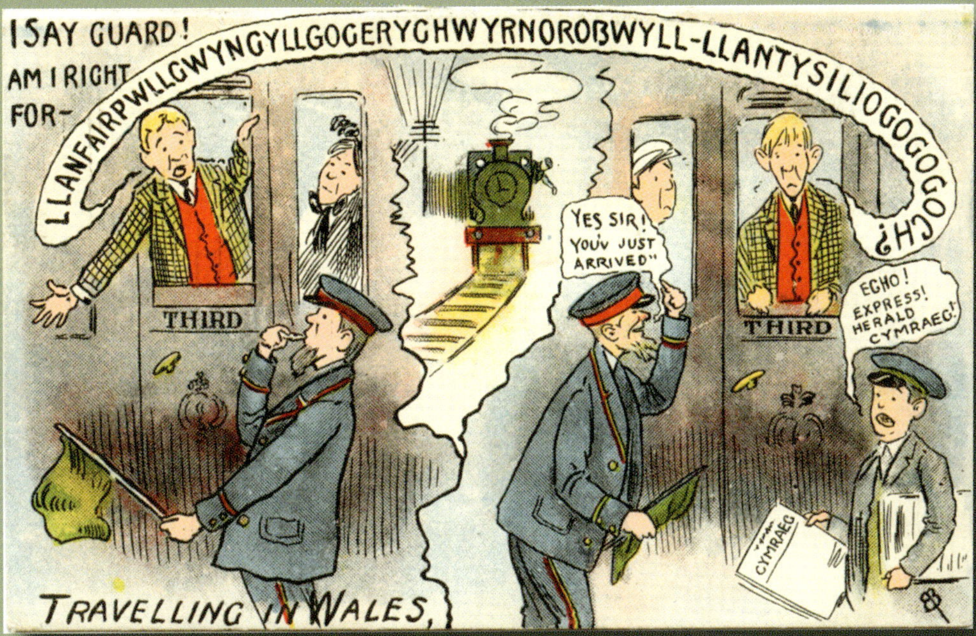
I SAY GUARD!
AM I RIGHT FOR-
LLANFAIRPWLLGWYNGYLLGOGERYCHWYRNOROBWYLL-LLANTYSILIOGOGOGOCH?
YES SIR! YOU'V JUST ARRIVED"
ECHO! EXPRESS! HERALD CYMRAEG!
THIRD
THIRD
CYMRAEG
TRAVELLING IN WALES.

No. 230

No. 204

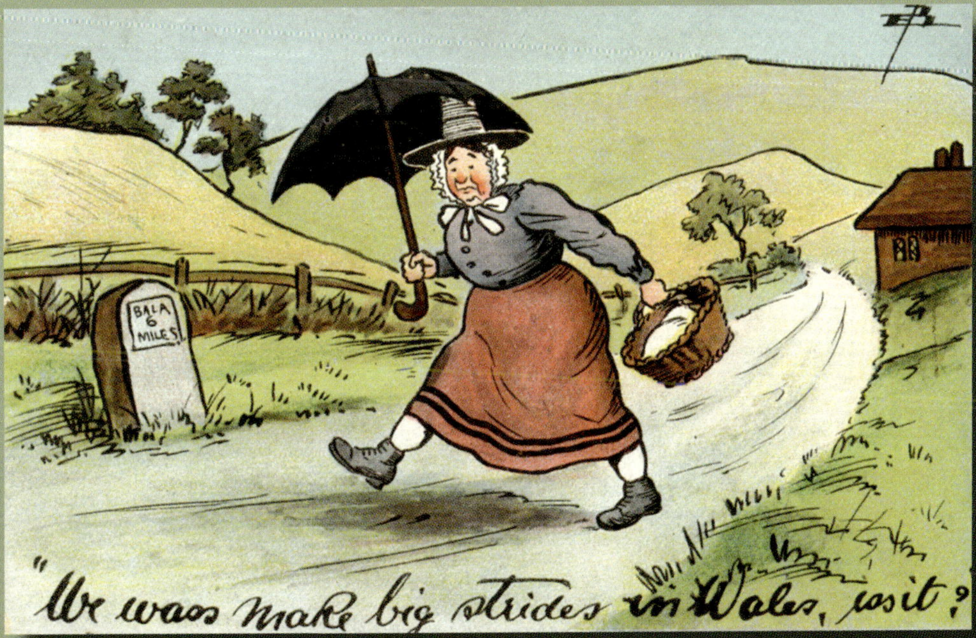
BALA 6 MILES
"We was make big strides in Wales, wsit?

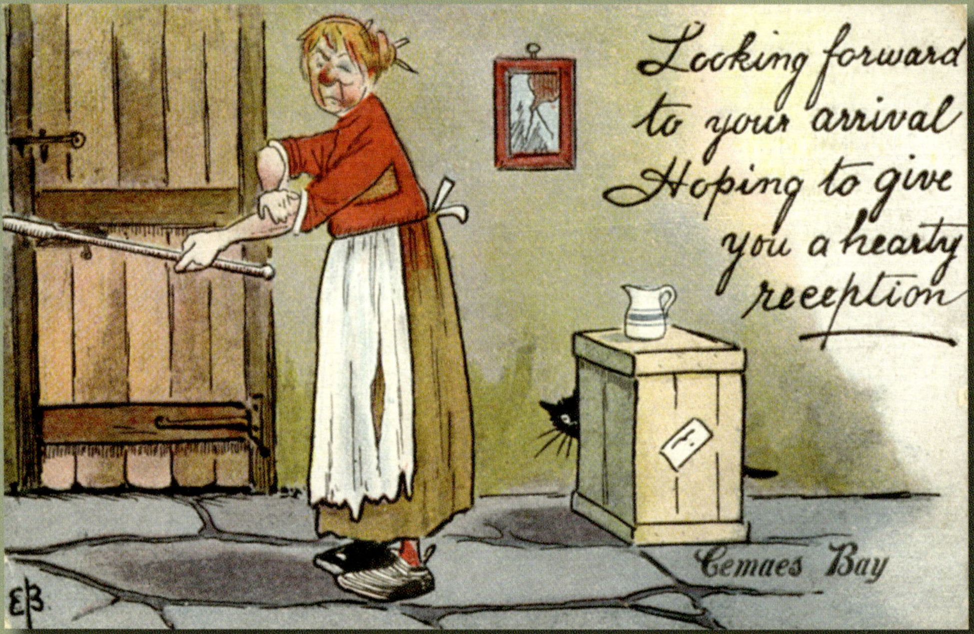
Looking forward
to your arrival
Hoping to give
you a hearty
reception
Cemaes Bay

No. 422

No. 409

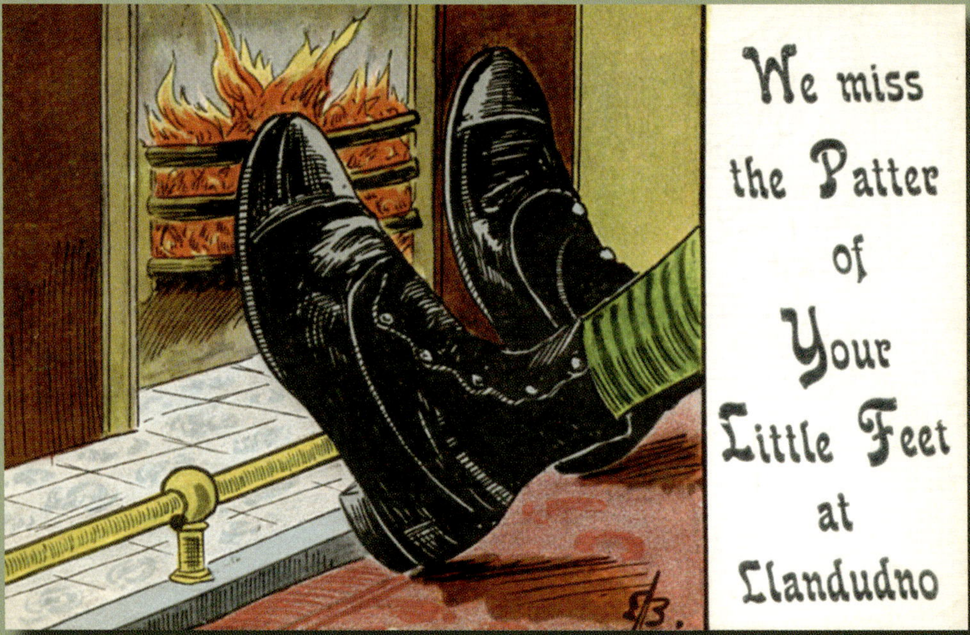
We miss
the Patter
of
Your
Little Feet
at
Llandudno

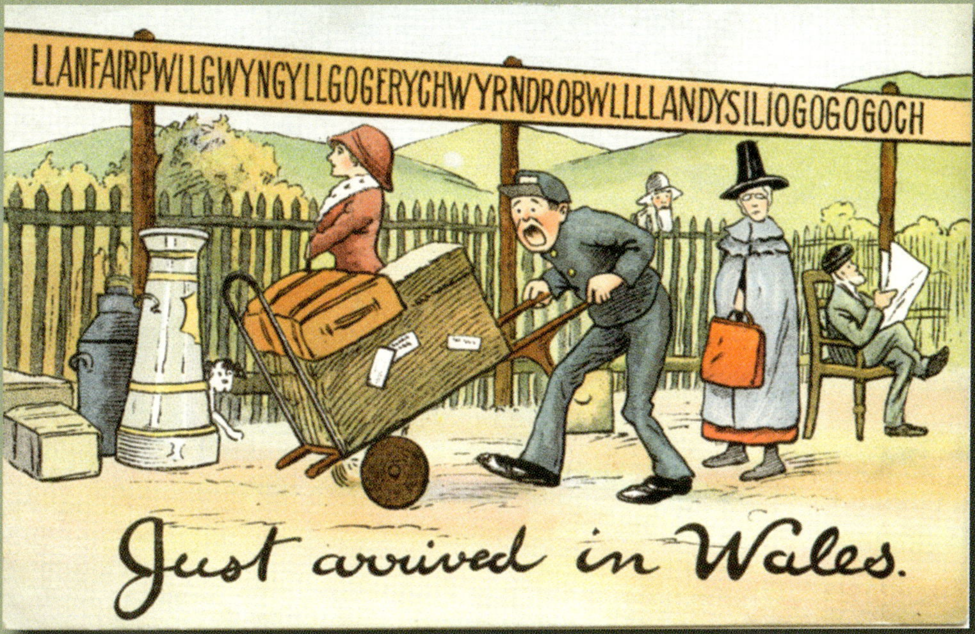

No. 2903

No. 425

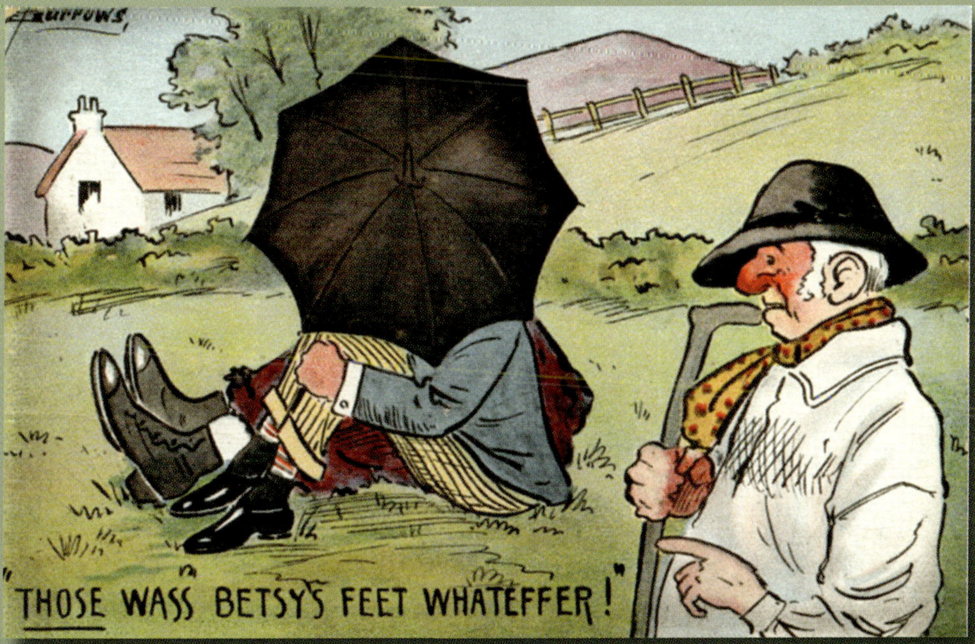

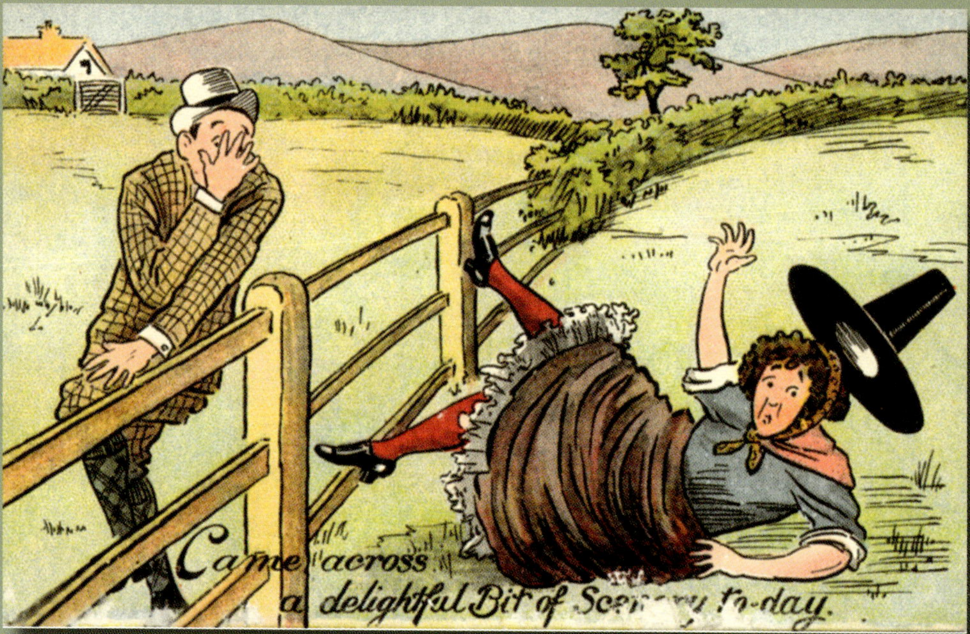

No. 204

No. 3911

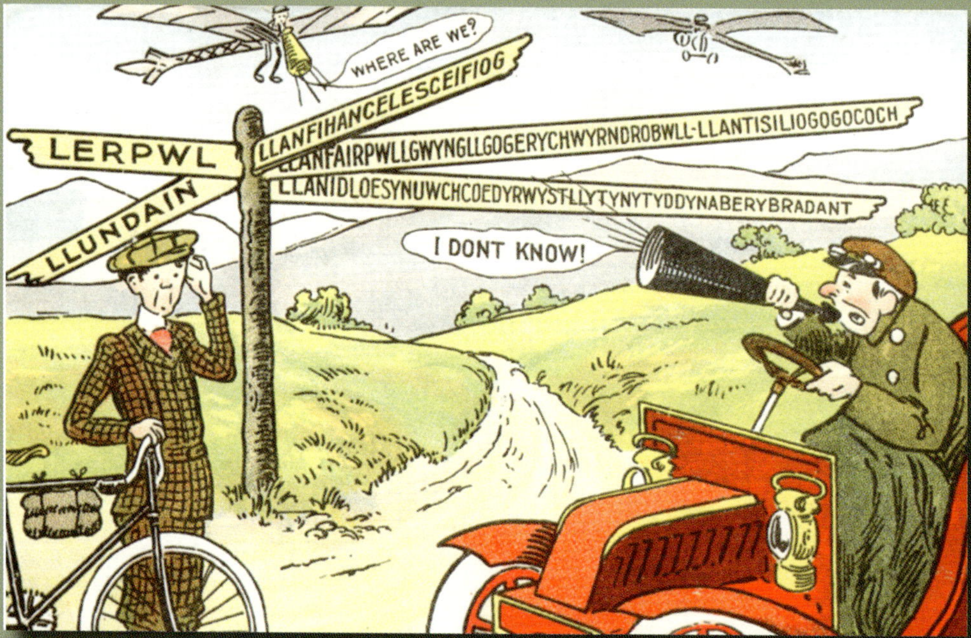

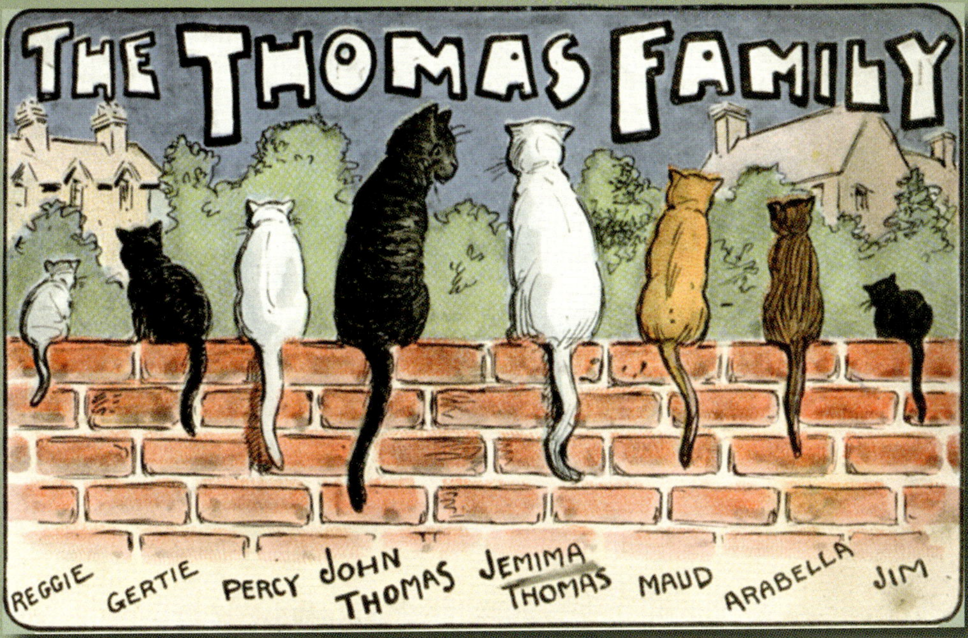
THE THOMAS FAMILY
REGGIE
GERTIE
PERCY
JOHN THOMAS
JEMIMA THOMAS
MAUD
ARABELLA
JIM

No. 523

No. 231

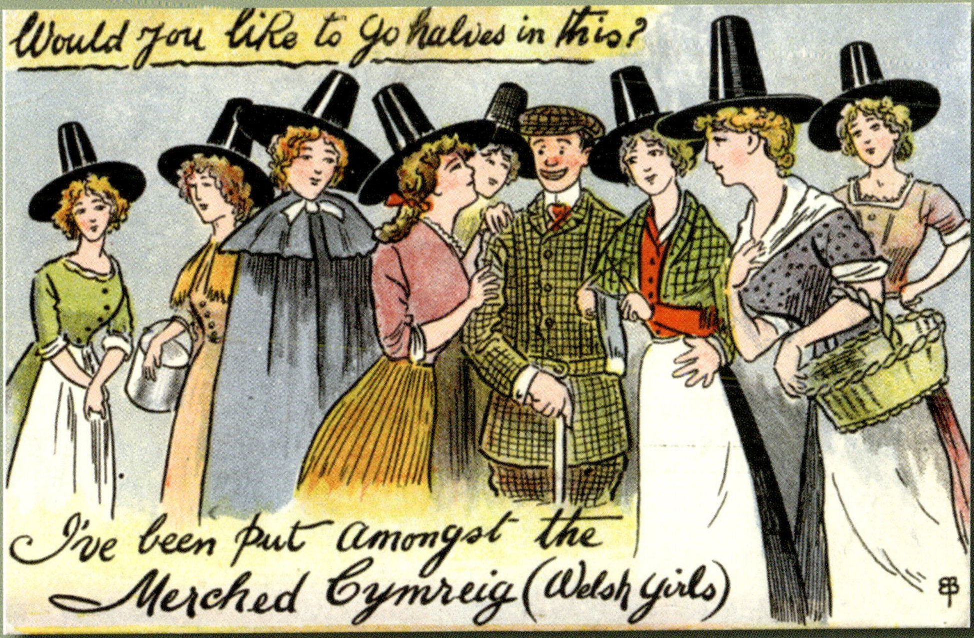
Would you like to go halves in this?
I've been put amongst the
Merched Cymreig (Welsh girls)

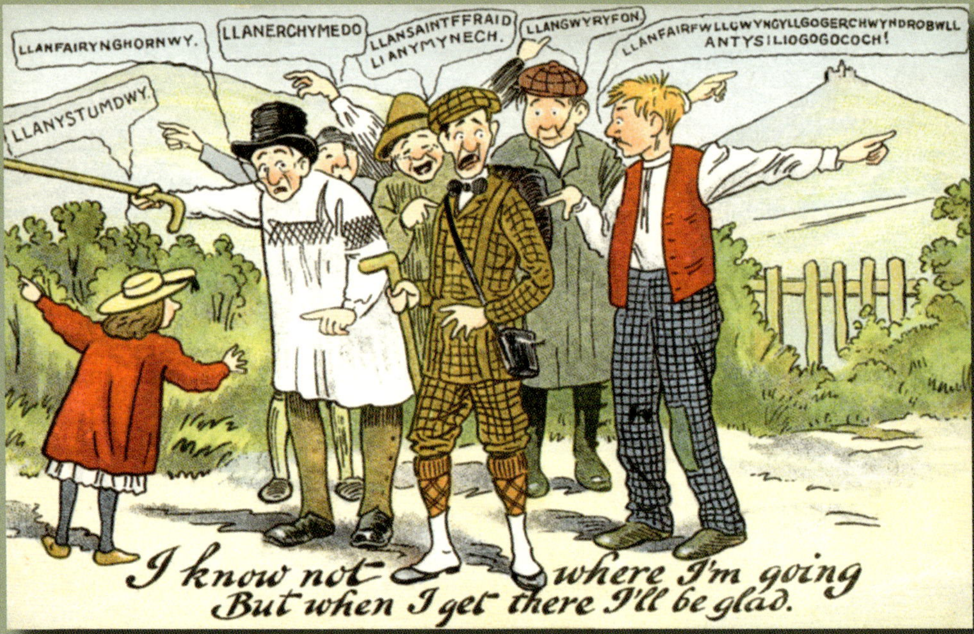

No. 3008

No. 202

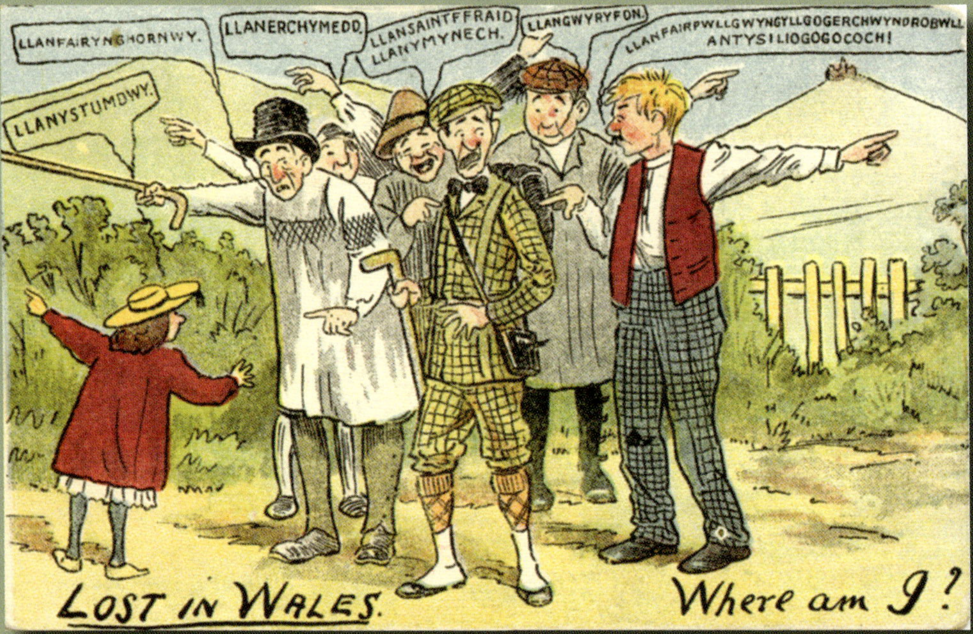

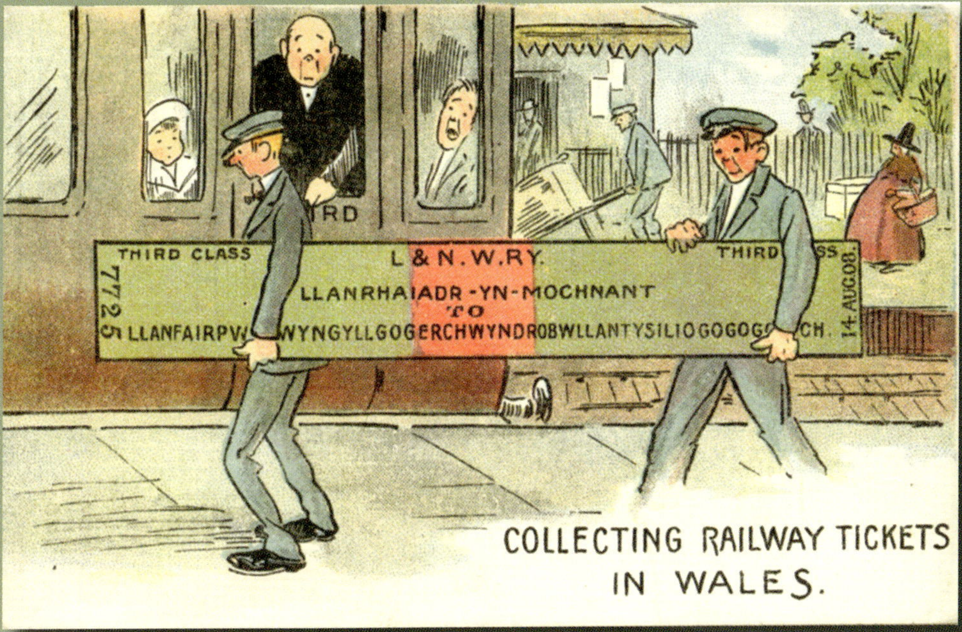
RD
THIRD CLASS
L & N. W. RY.
THIRD
7725
LLANRHAIADR-YN-MOCHNANT
TO
LLANFAIRPW
WYNGYLLGOGERCHWYNDROBWLLANTYSILIOGOGOG
CH.
14-AUG08
COLLECTING RAILWAY TICKETS
IN WALES.

No. 201

No. 201

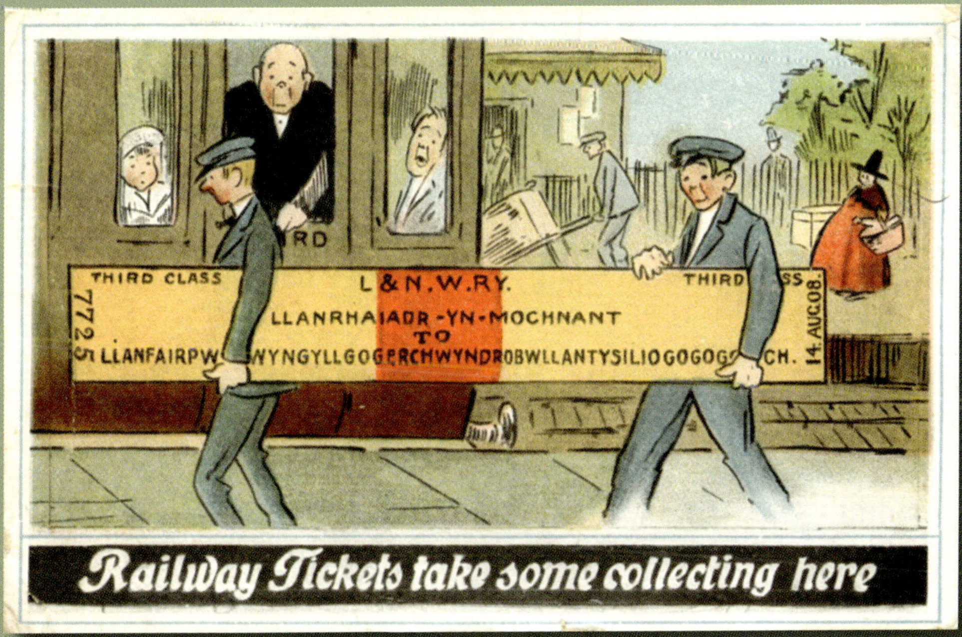
RD
THIRD CLASS
L & N. W. RY.
THIRD
7725
LLANRHAIADR-YN-MOCHNANT
TO
LLANFAIRPW
WYNGYLLGOGERCHWYNDROBWLLANTYSILIOGOGOG
CH.
14 AUG08
Railway Tickets take some collecting here

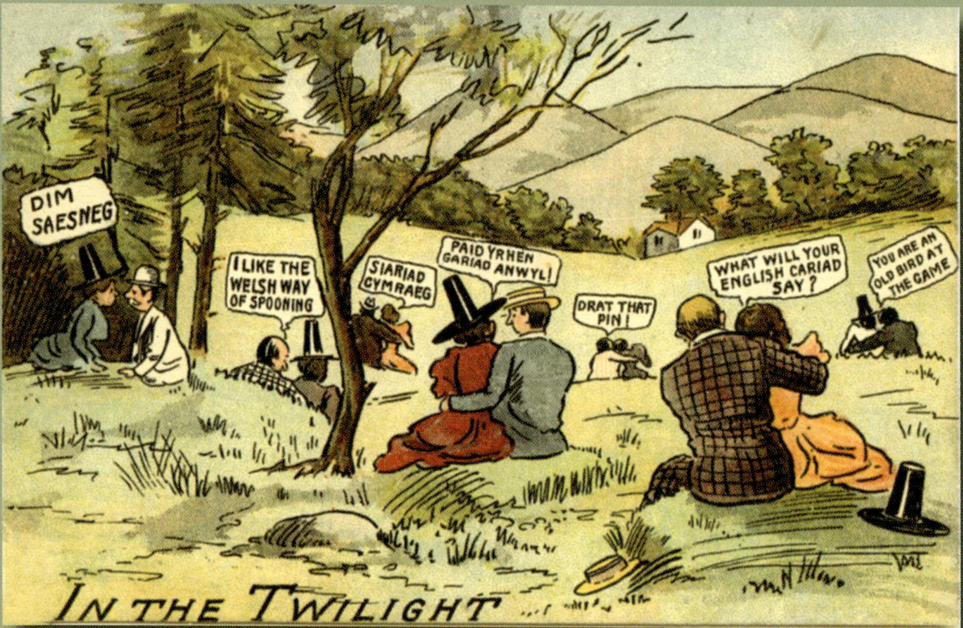

No. 208

No. 3604

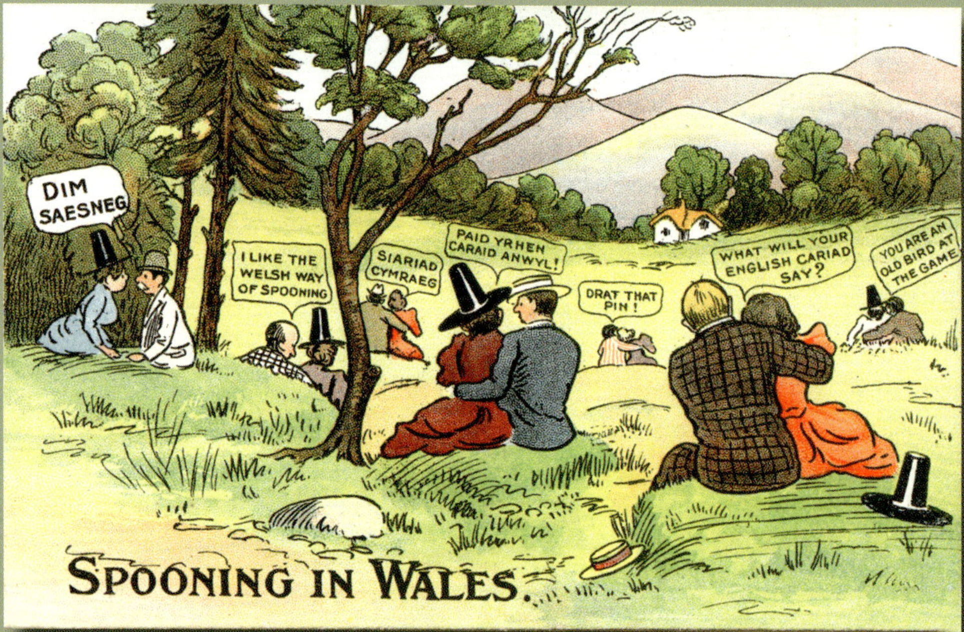

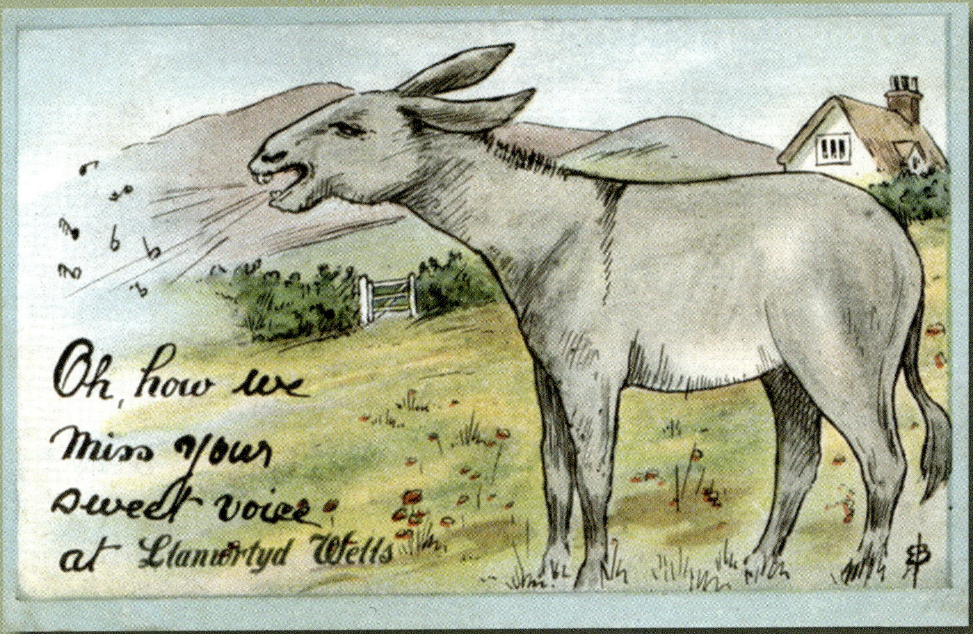
Oh, how we
miss your
sweet voice
at Llanwrtyd Wells

No. 550

No. 424

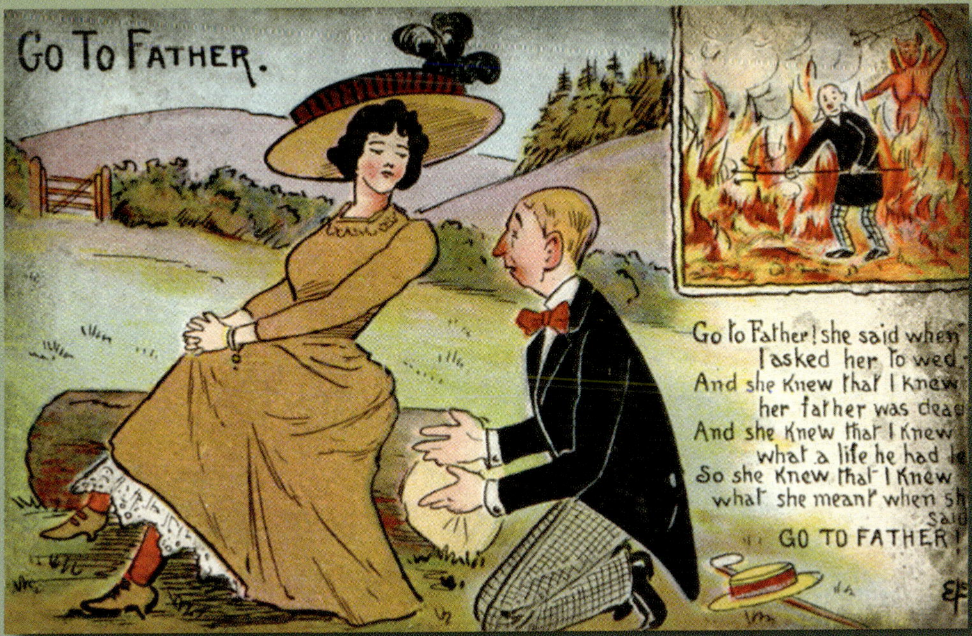
GO TO FATHER.
Go to Father! she said when
I asked her to wed.
And she knew that I knew
her father was dea
And she knew that I knew
what a life he had
So she knew that I knew
what she meant when sh
said
GO TO FATHER!

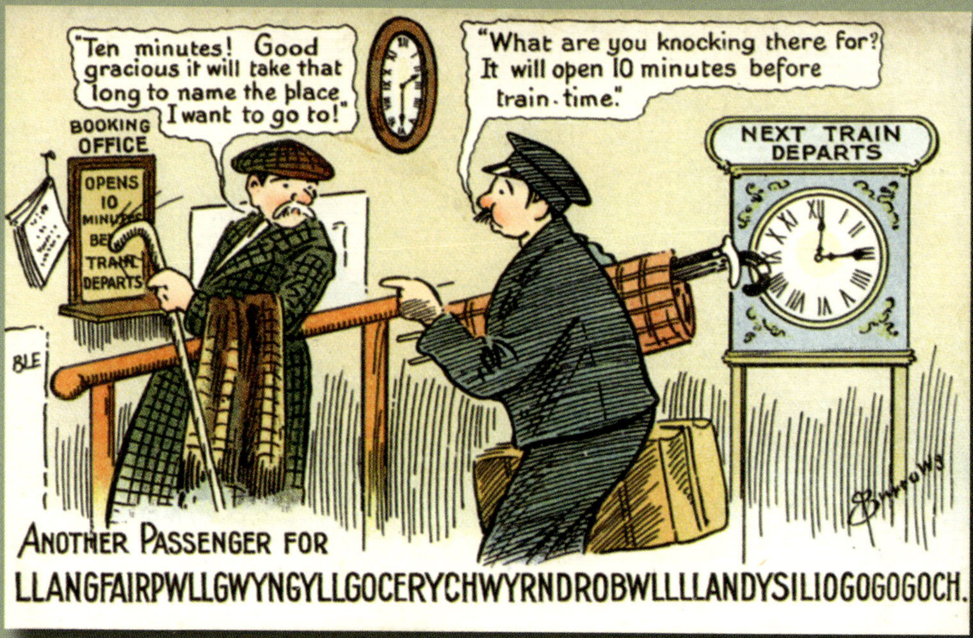

No. 2600

No. 423

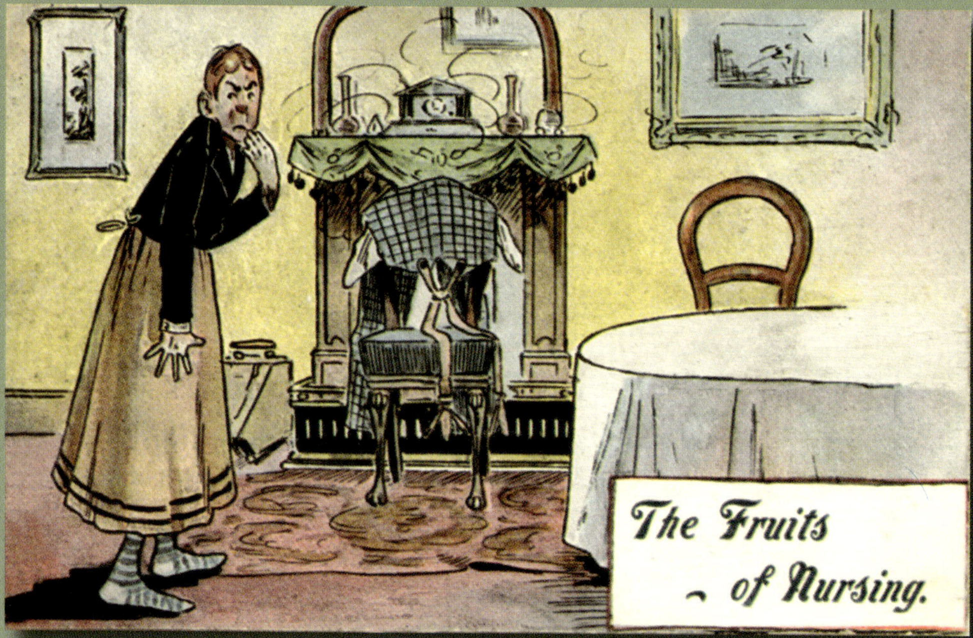

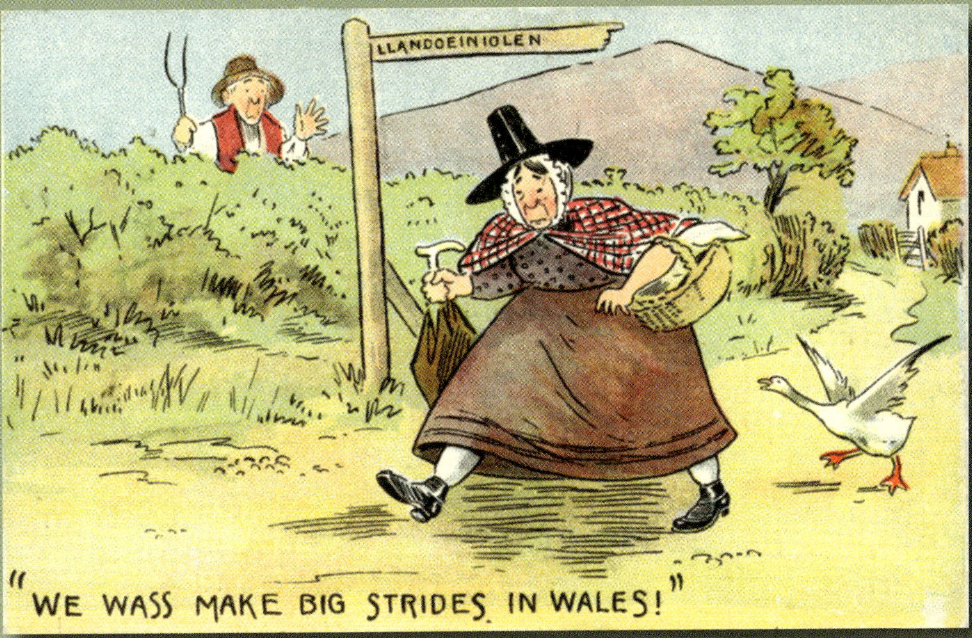
LLANDOEINIOLEN
"WE WASS MAKE BIG STRIDES IN WALES!"

Nº. 203

Nº. 233

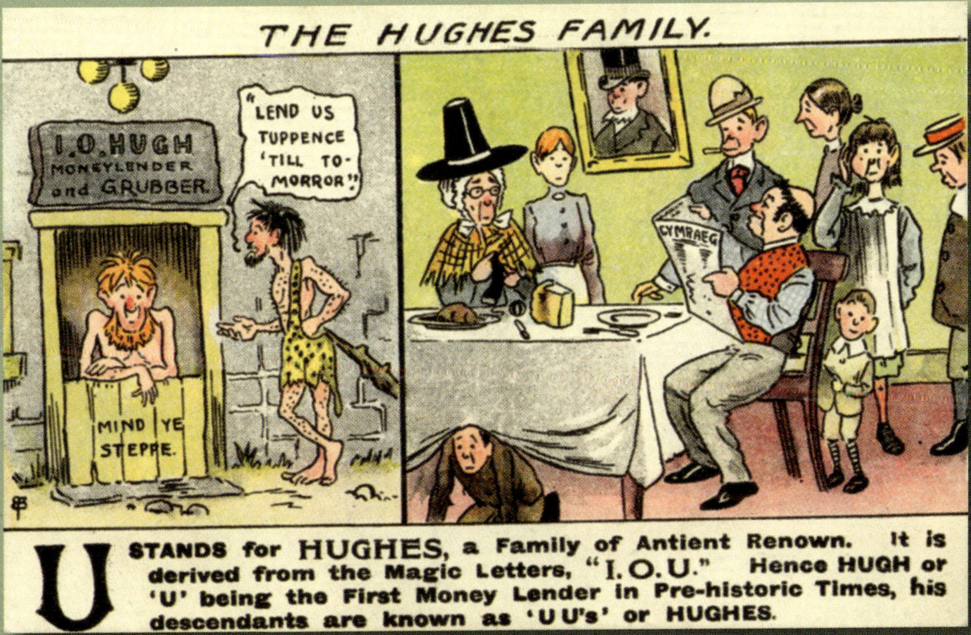
THE HUGHES FAMILY.
I.O. HUGH MONEYLENDER and GRUBBER
"LEND US TUPPENCE 'TILL TO-MORROR!"
MIND YE STEPPE.
CYMRAEG
U STANDS for HUGHES, a Family of Antient Renown. It is derived from the Magic Letters, "I.O.U." Hence HUGH or 'U' being the First Money Lender in Pre-historic Times, his descendants are known as 'U U's' or HUGHES.

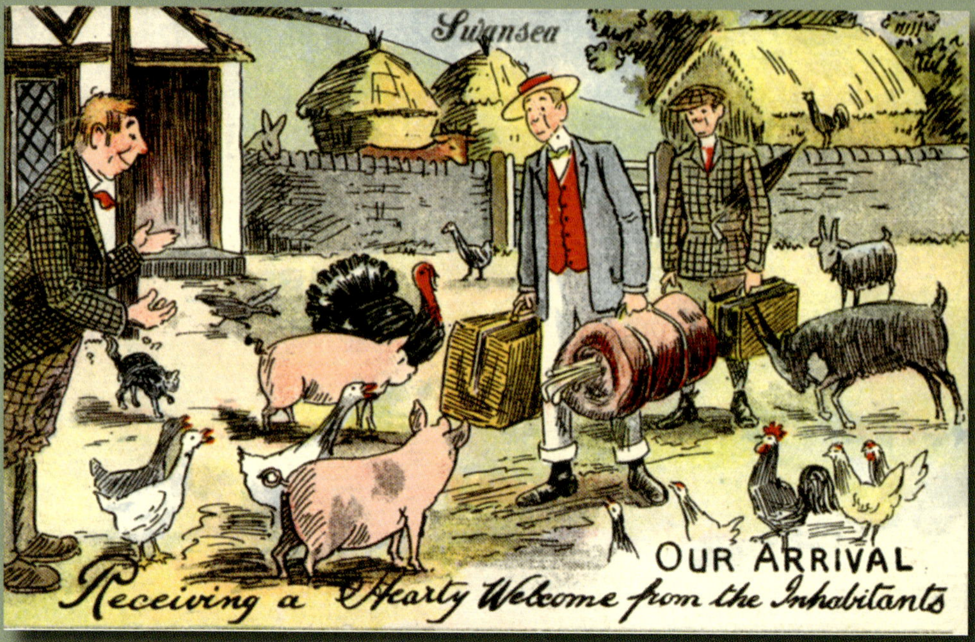
Swansea
OUR ARRIVAL
Receiving a Hearty Welcome from the Inhabitants

Nº. 241

Nº. 453

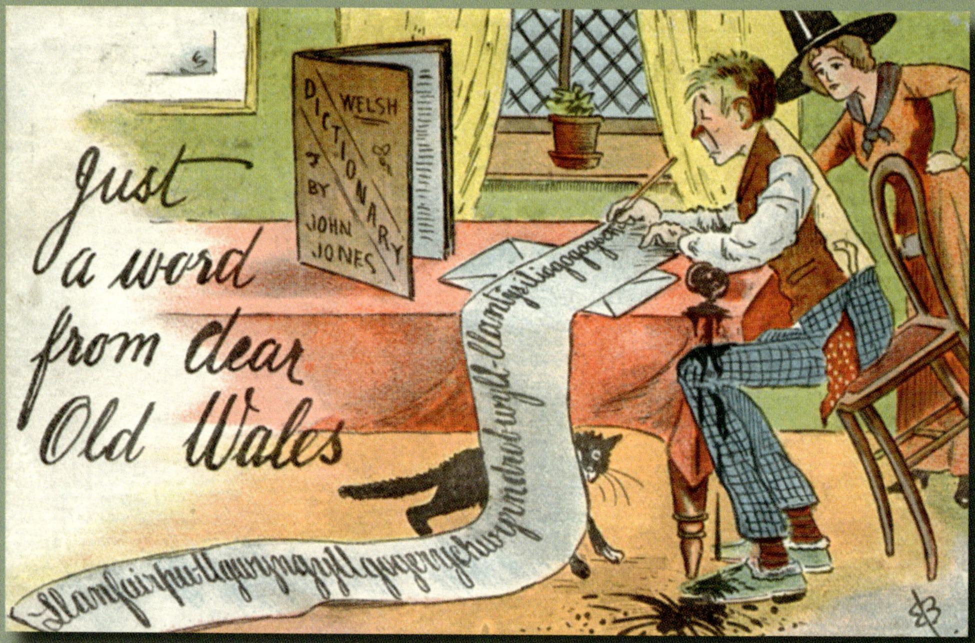
WELSH DICTIONARY BY JOHN JONES
Just a word from dear Old Wales

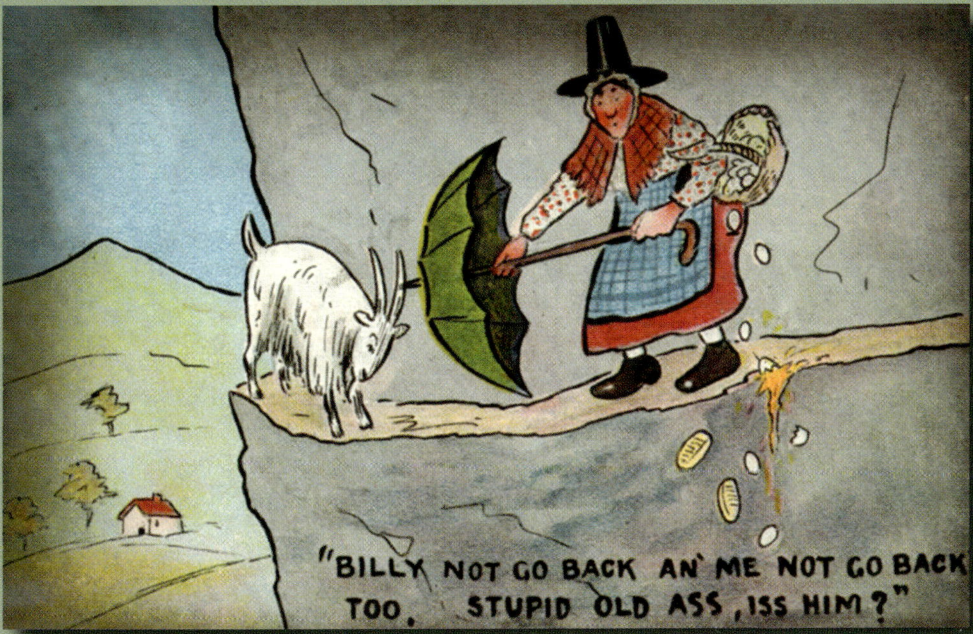
"BILLY NOT GO BACK AN' ME NOT GO BACK TOO, STUPID OLD ASS, ISS HIM?"

No. 458

No. 235

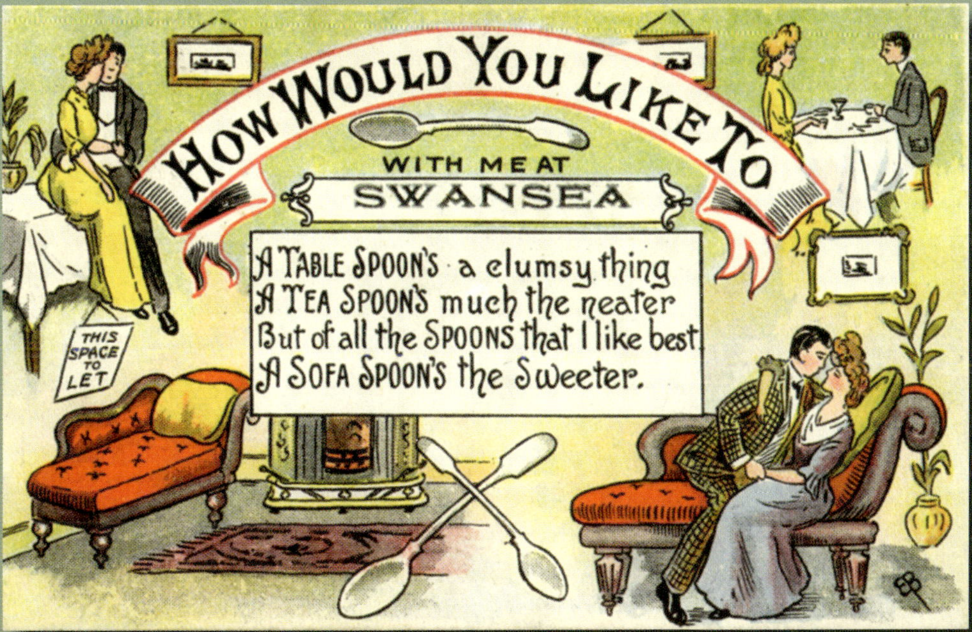
HOW WOULD YOU LIKE TO
WITH ME AT
SWANSEA
A TABLE SPOON'S a clumsy thing
A TEA SPOON'S much the neater
But of all the SPOONS that I like best
A SOFA SPOON'S the Sweeter.
THIS SPACE TO LET

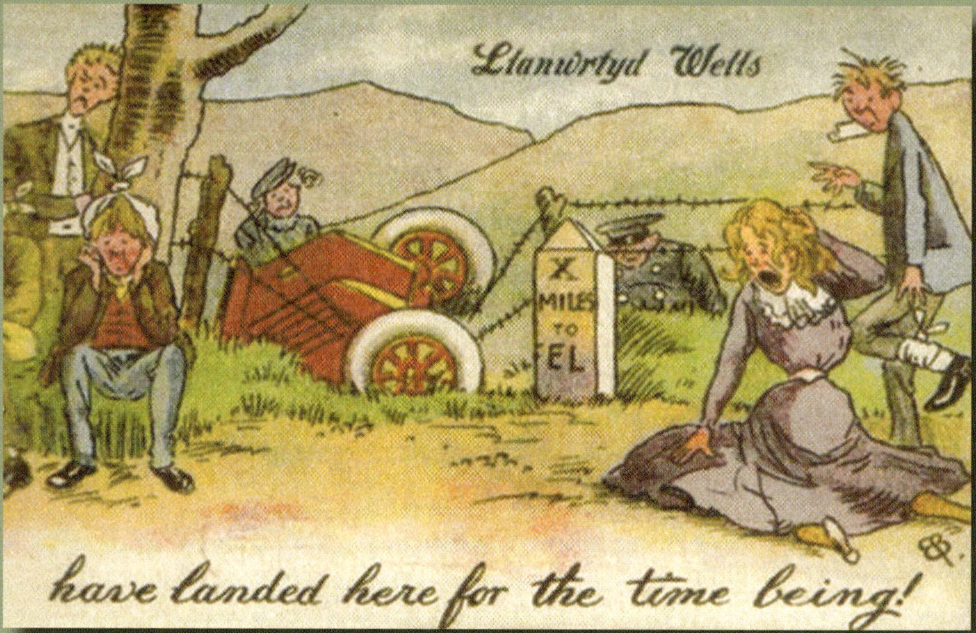

Nº. 236

Nº. Not numbered

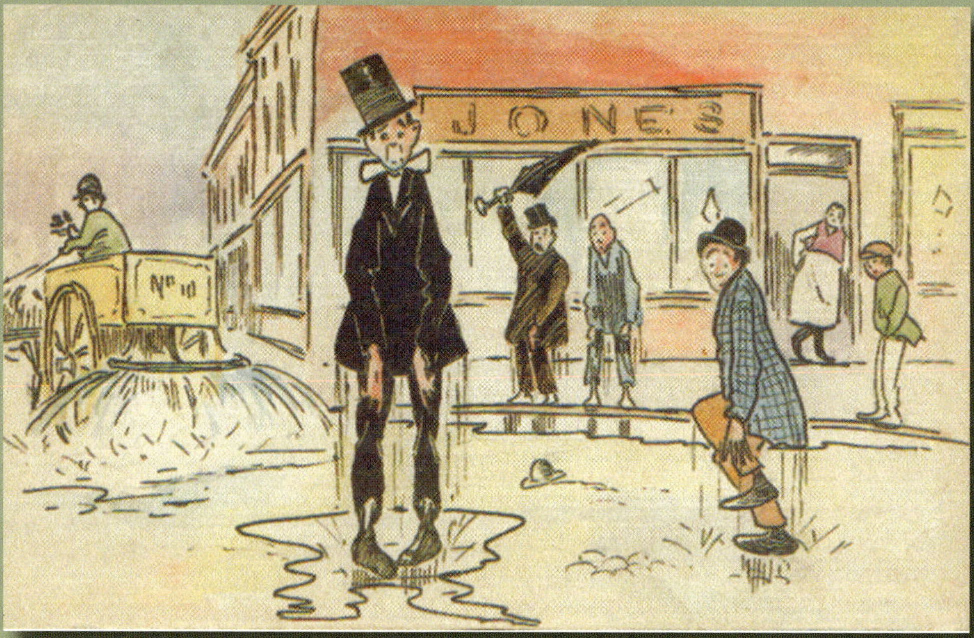

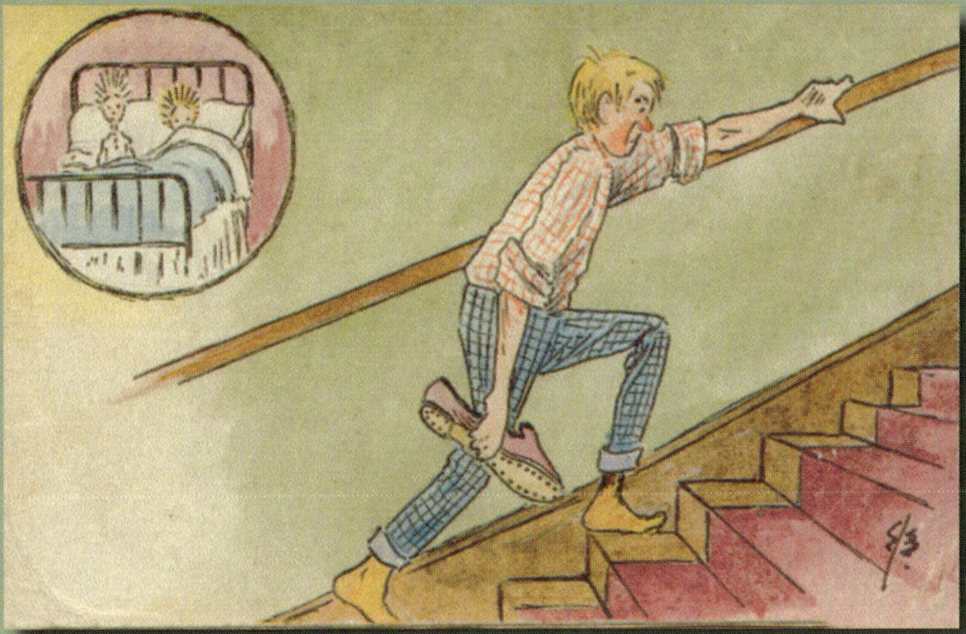

N^o. Not numbered

N°. 237

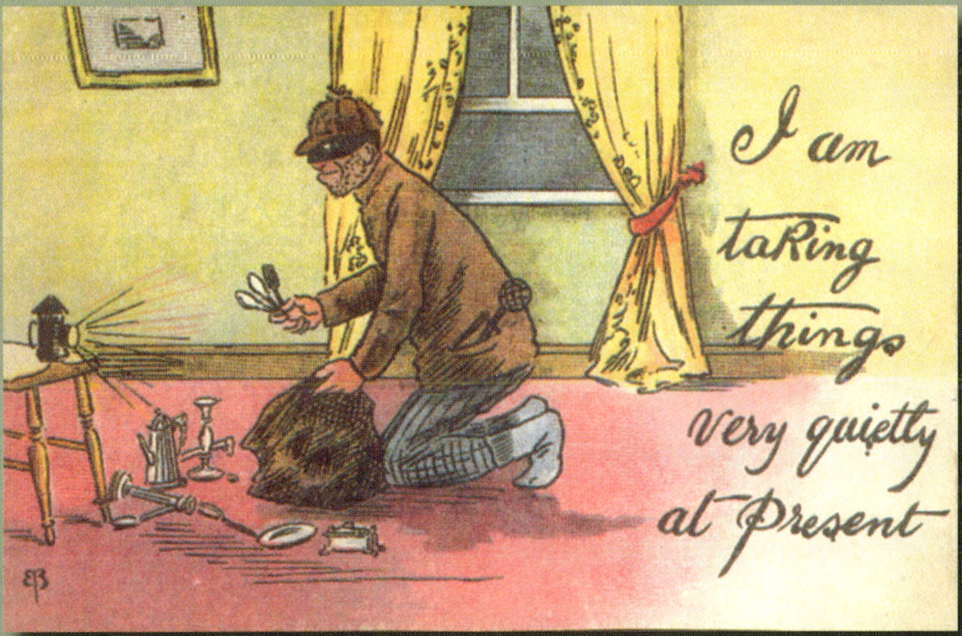

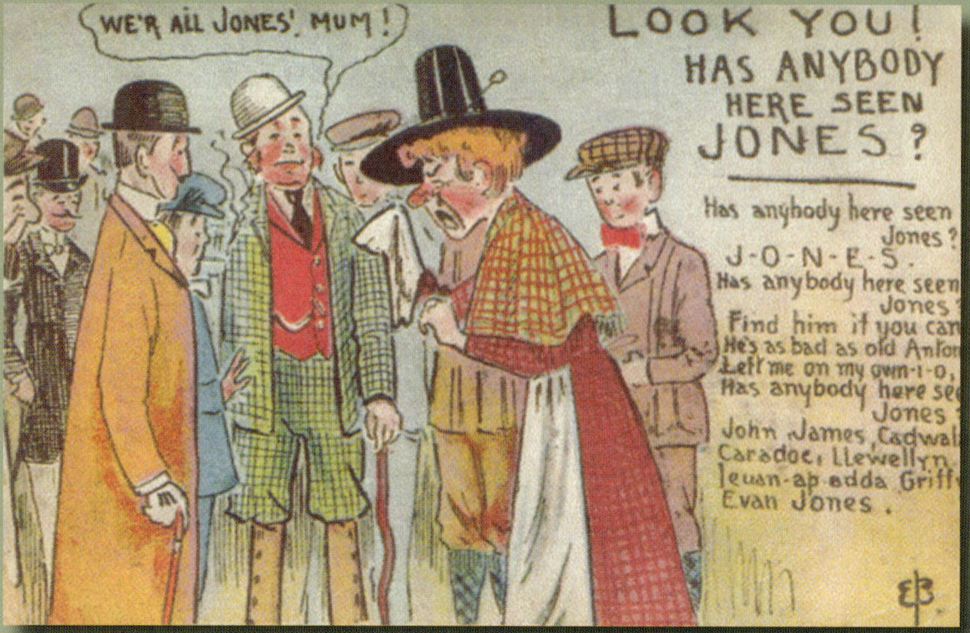
WE'R ALL JONES! MUM!
LOOK YOU!
HAS ANYBODY HERE SEEN JONES?
Has anybody here seen Jones?
J-O-N-E-S.
Has anybody here seen Jones
Find him if you can
He's as bad as old Anto
Left me on my own-i-o,
Has anybody here see
Jones
John James Cadwal
Caradoc, Llewellyn
Ieuan-ap-adda Griff
Evan Jones.
EB

Nº. 455

Nº. 238

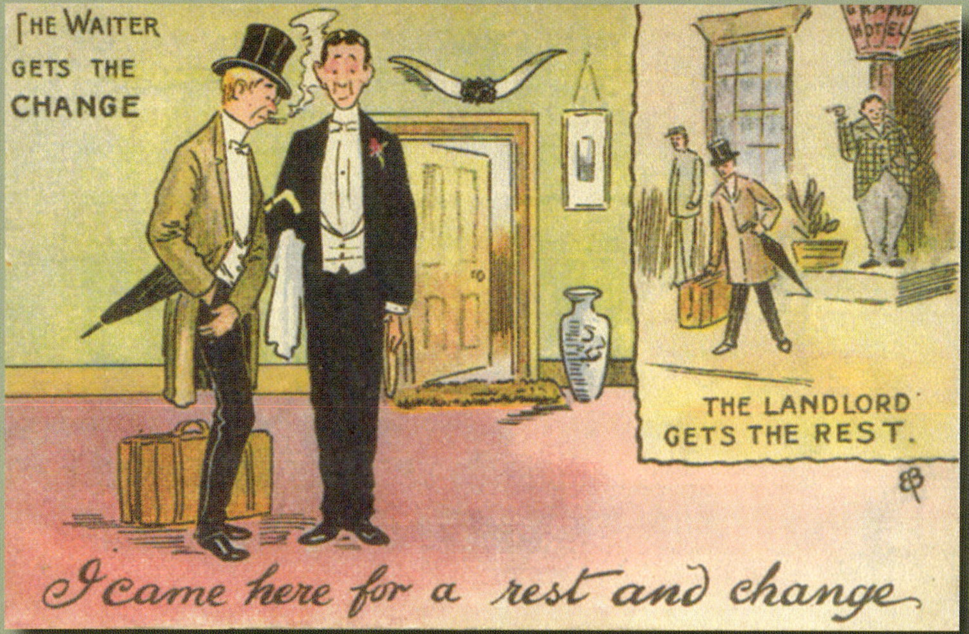
THE WAITER GETS THE CHANGE
GRAND HOTEL
THE LANDLORD GETS THE REST.
EB
I came here for a rest and change

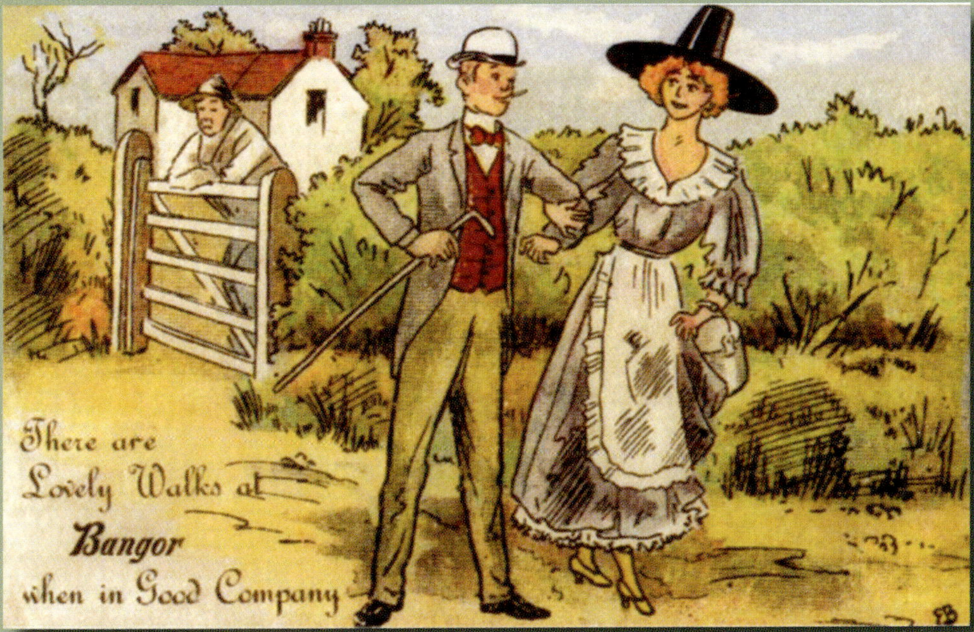
There are
Lovely Walks at
Bangor
when in Good Company
EB

No. 227

No. 420

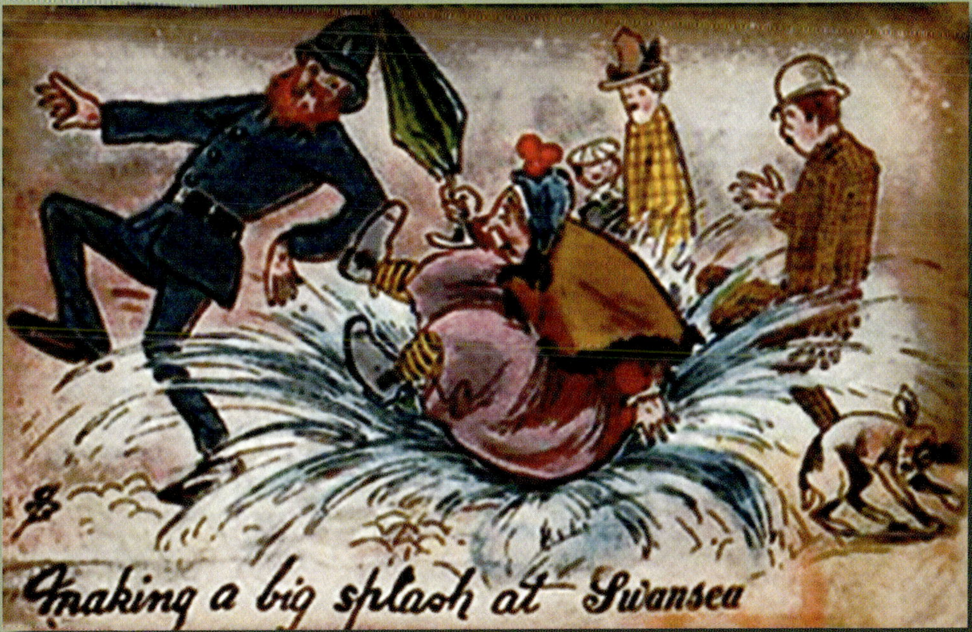
Making a big splash at Swansea

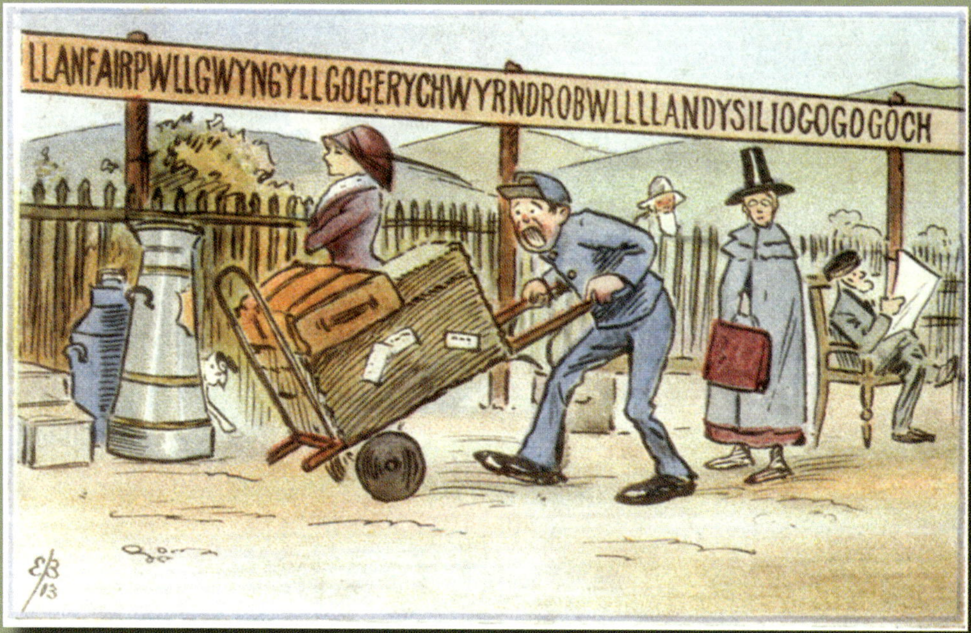
LLANFAIRPWLLGWYNGYLLGOGERYCHWYRNDROBWLLLLANDYSILIOGOGOGOCH

N°. 527

N°. 412

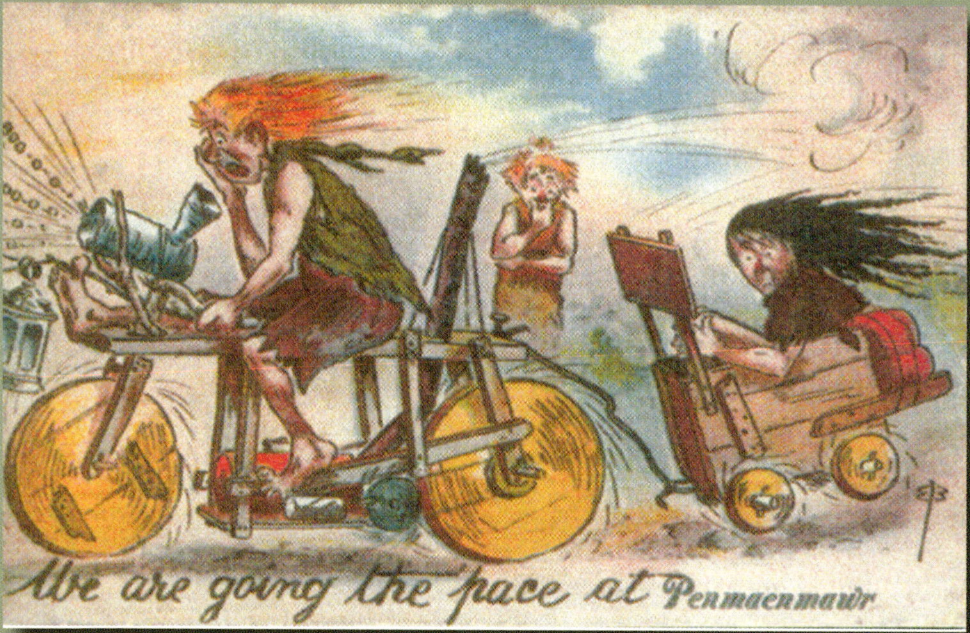
We are going the pace at Penmaenmawr

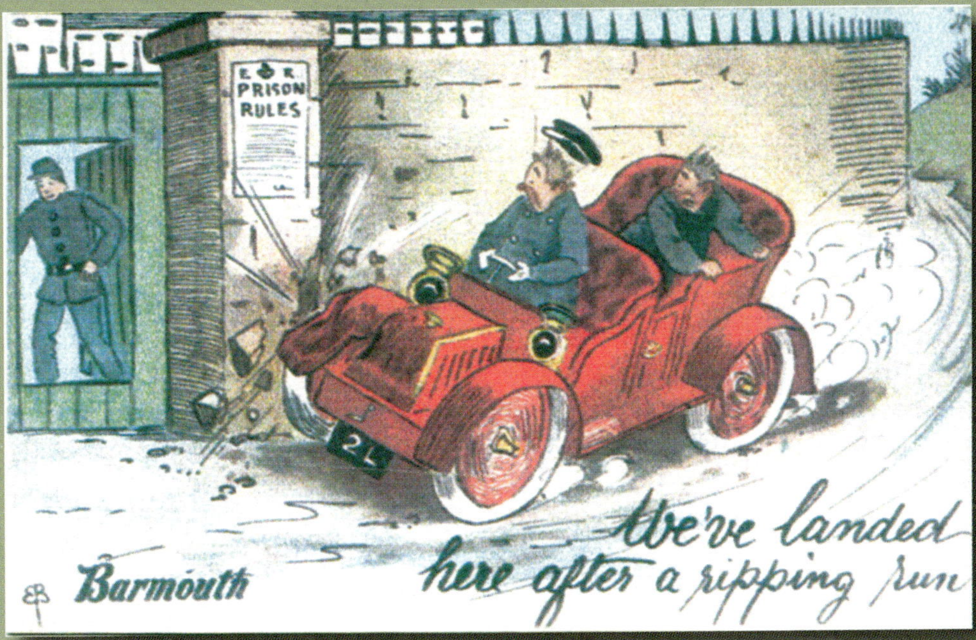
PRISON
RULES
We've landed
here after a ripping run
Barmouth

No. 413

No. 415

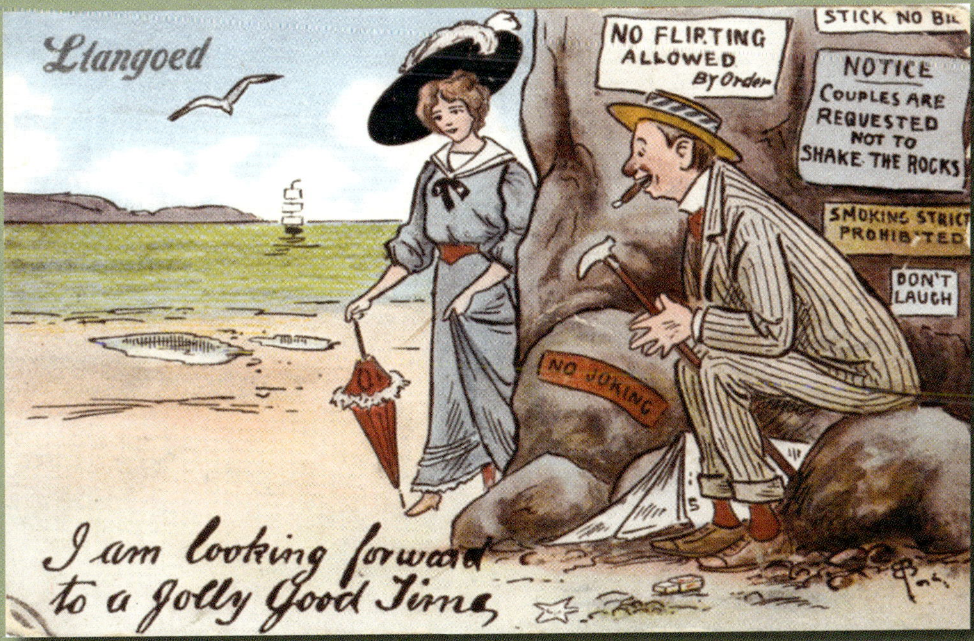
Llangoed
NO FLIRTING
ALLOWED
By Order
STICK NO BIL
NOTICE
COUPLES ARE
REQUESTED
NOT TO
SHAKE THE ROCKS
SMOKING STRICT
PROHIBITED
DON'T
LAUGH
NO JOKING
I am looking forward
to a Jolly Good Time

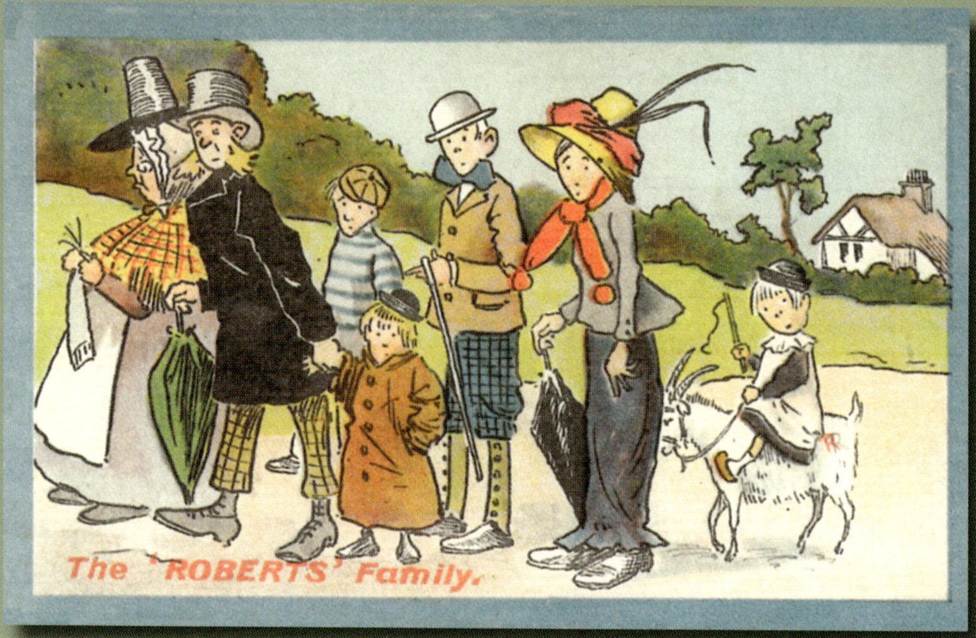
The 'ROBERTS' Family.

Nº. 522

Nº. 205

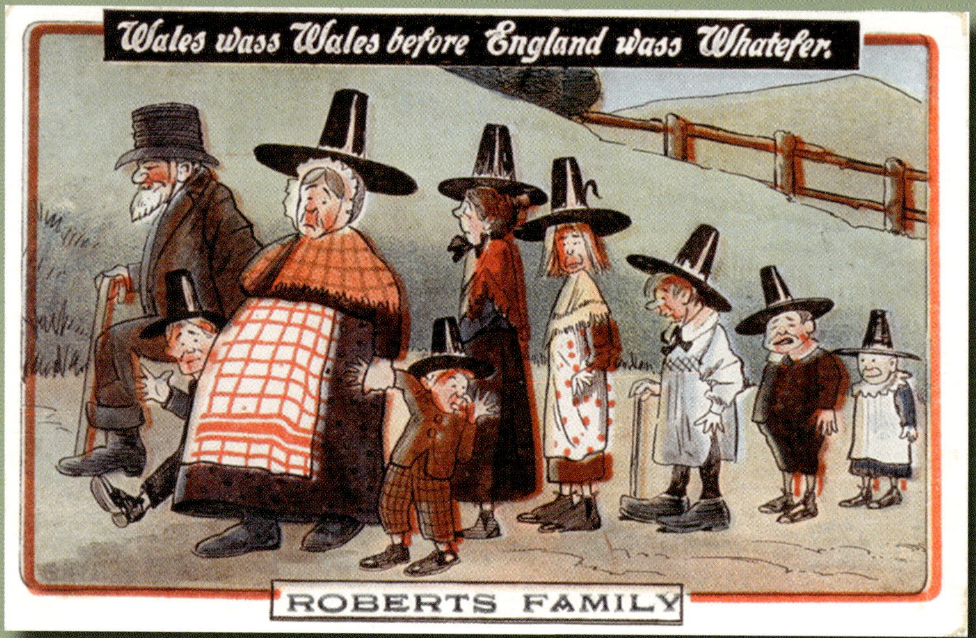
Wales wass Wales before England wass Whatefer.
ROBERTS FAMILY

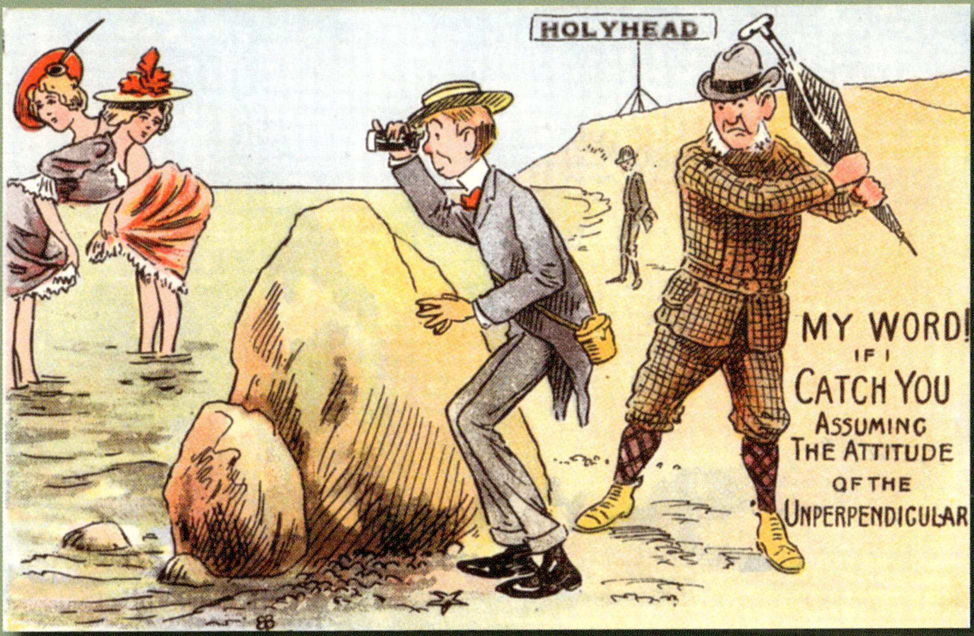
HOLYHEAD
MY WORD!
IF I
CATCH YOU
ASSUMING
THE ATTITUDE
OF THE
UNPERPENDICULAR

No. 240

No. 409

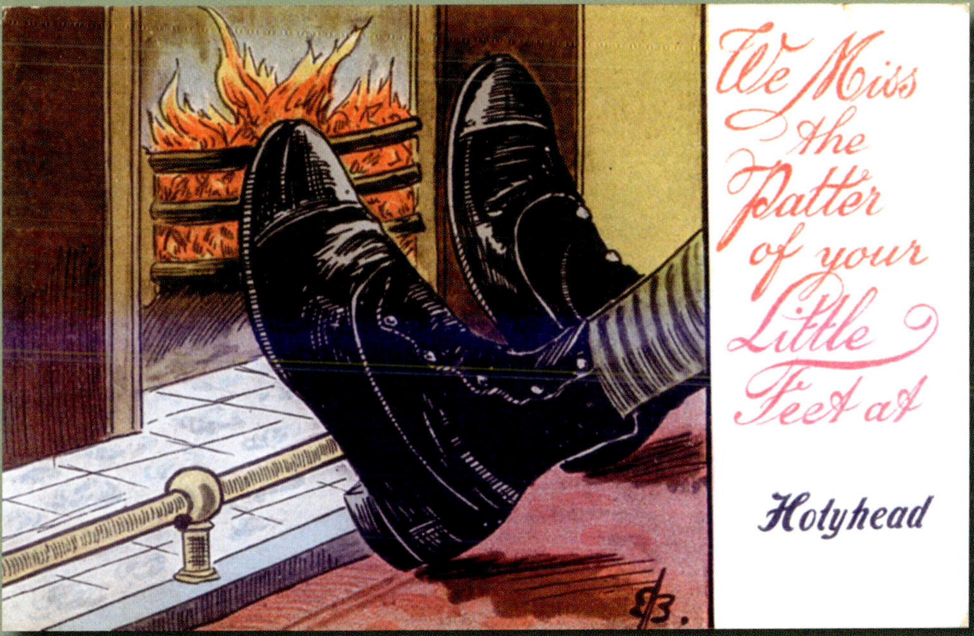
We Miss
the
Patter
of your
Little
Feet at
Holyhead

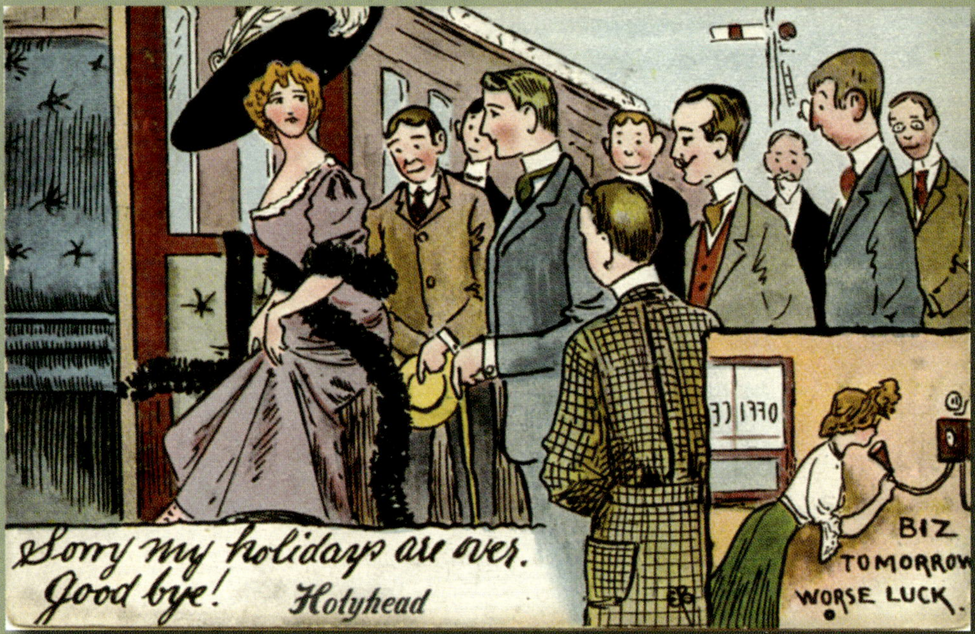
Sorry my holidays are over.
Good bye!
Holyhead
BIZ
TOMORROW
WORSE LUCK.

No. 417

No. 414

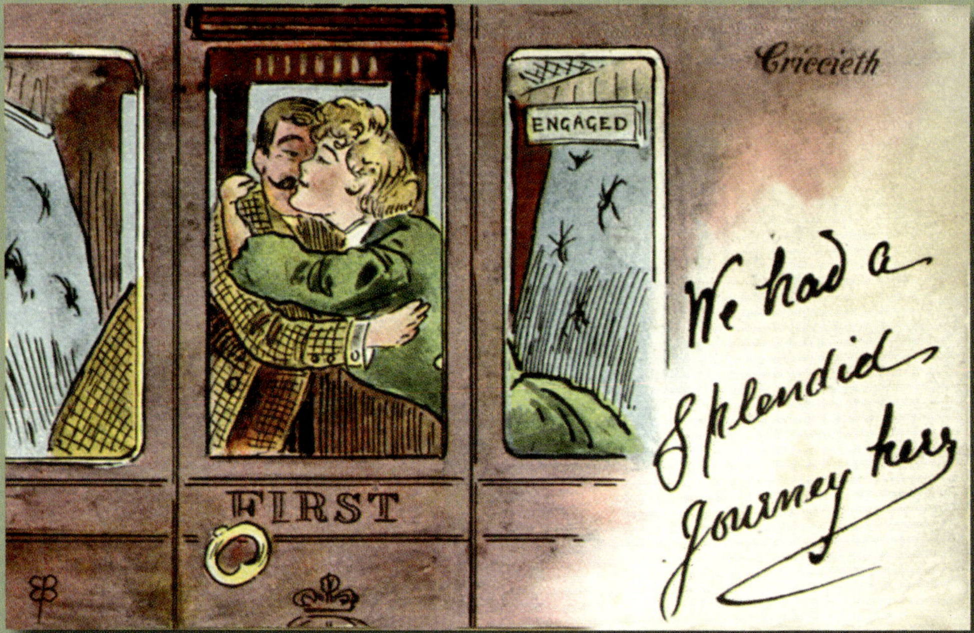
Criccieth
ENGAGED
FIRST
We had a
Splendid
Journey here

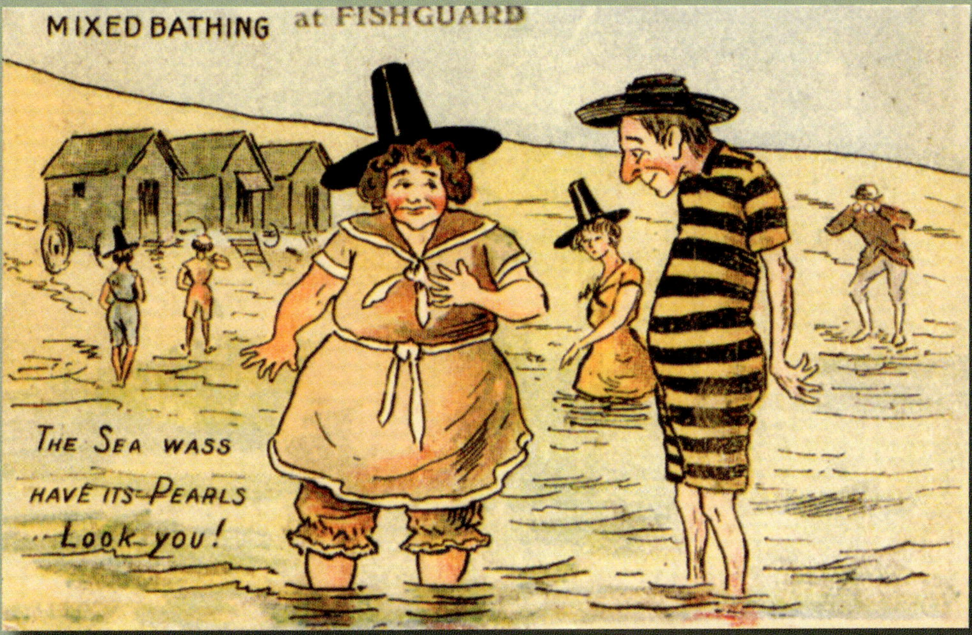
MIXED BATHING at FISHGUARD
THE SEA WASS HAVE ITS PEARLS Look you!

No. 215

No. 418

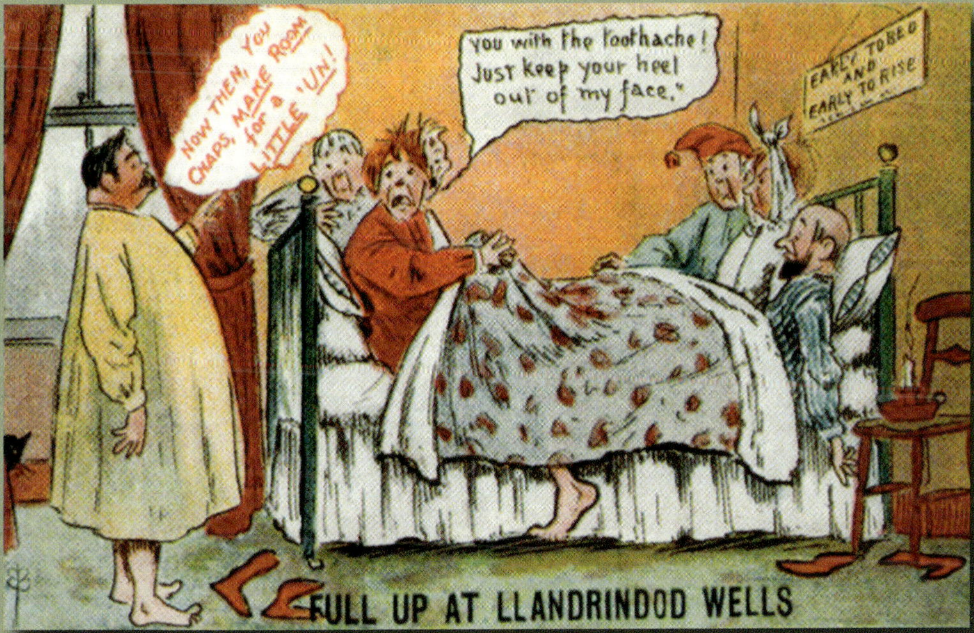
NOW THEN, YOU CHAPS, MAKE ROOM for a LITTLE 'UN!
You with the toothache! Just keep your heel out of my face."
EARLY TO BED AND EARLY TO RISE
FULL UP AT LLANDRINDOD WELLS

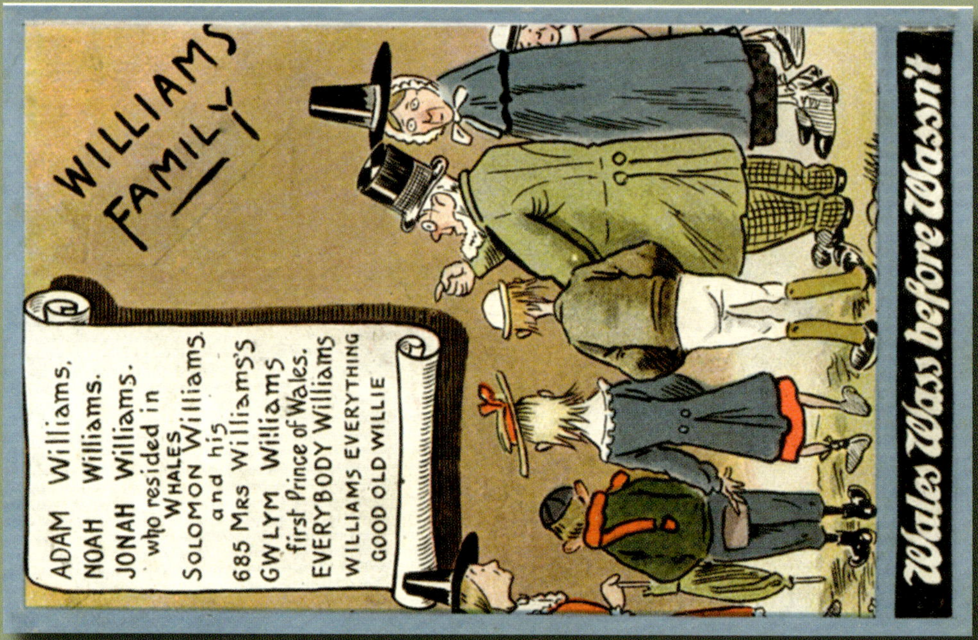

No. 242

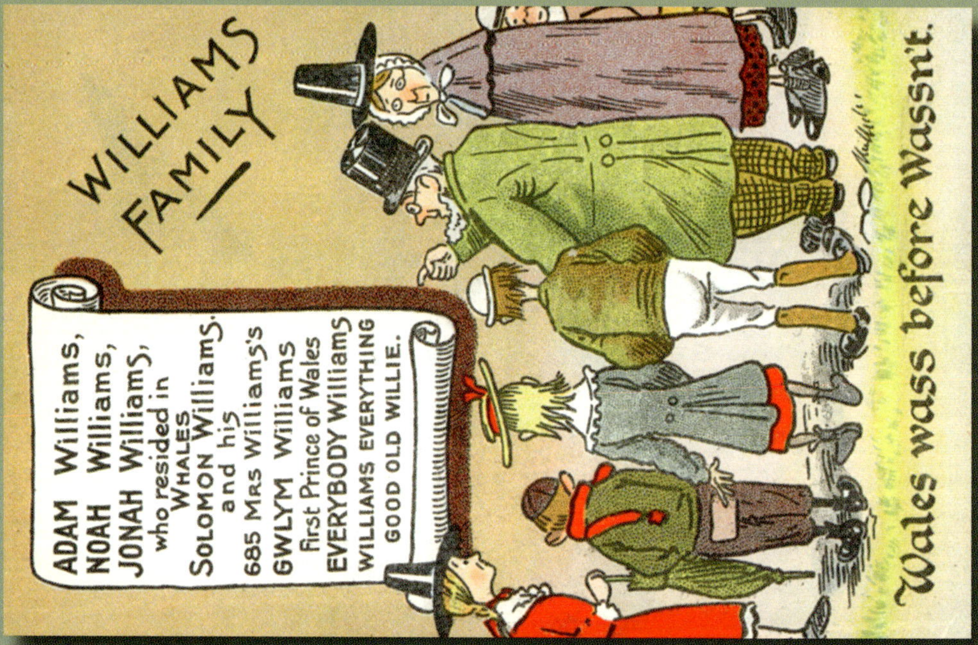

No. 3803

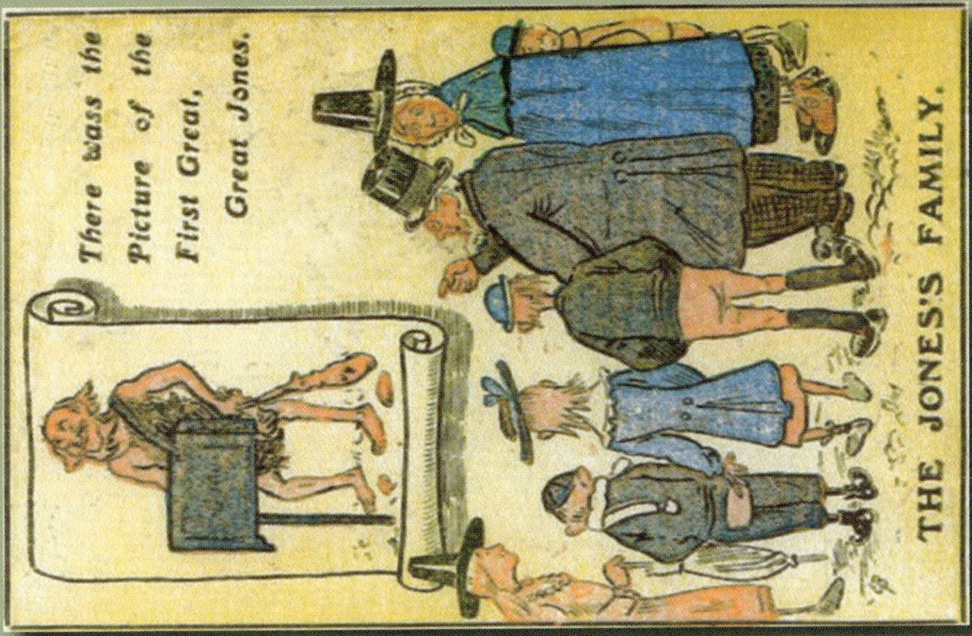

No. Not numbered

No. 1009

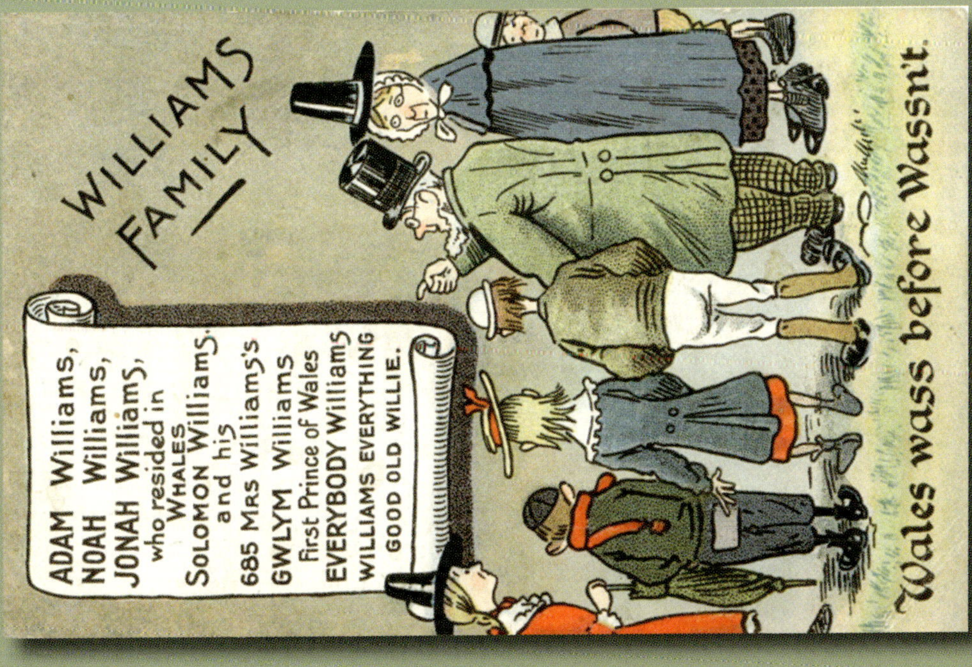

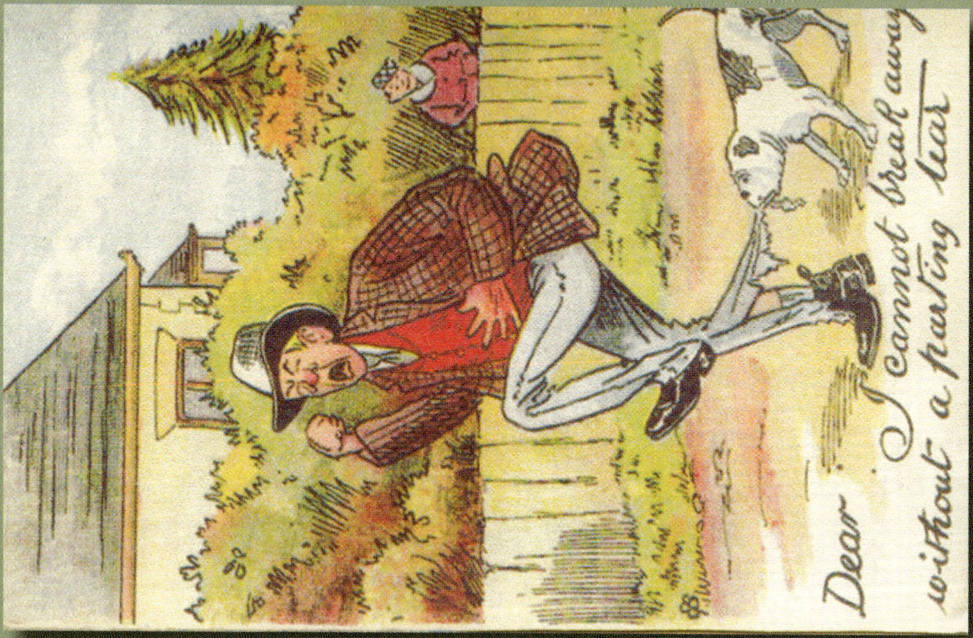

No. 239

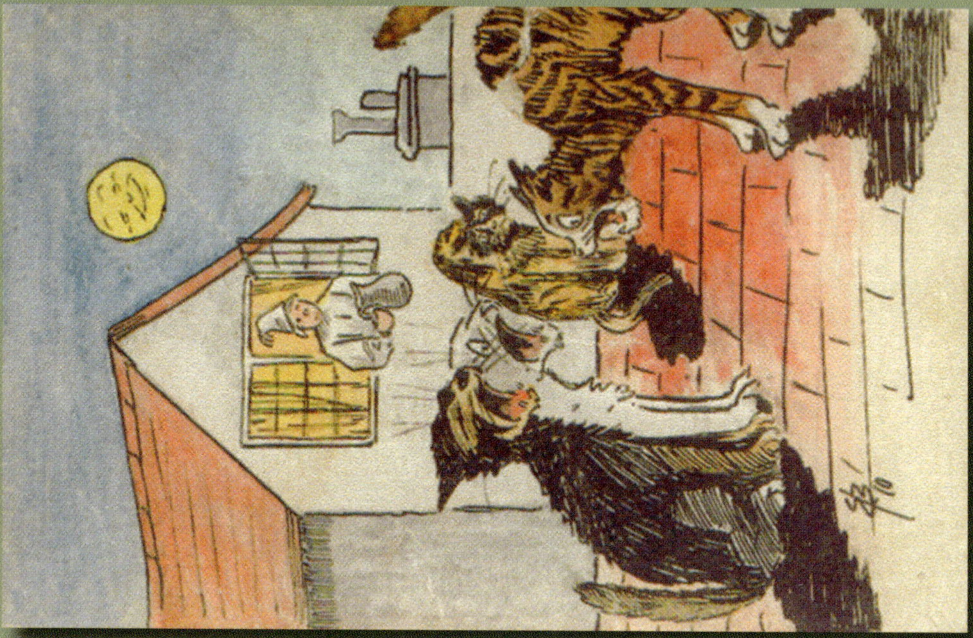

No. Not numbered

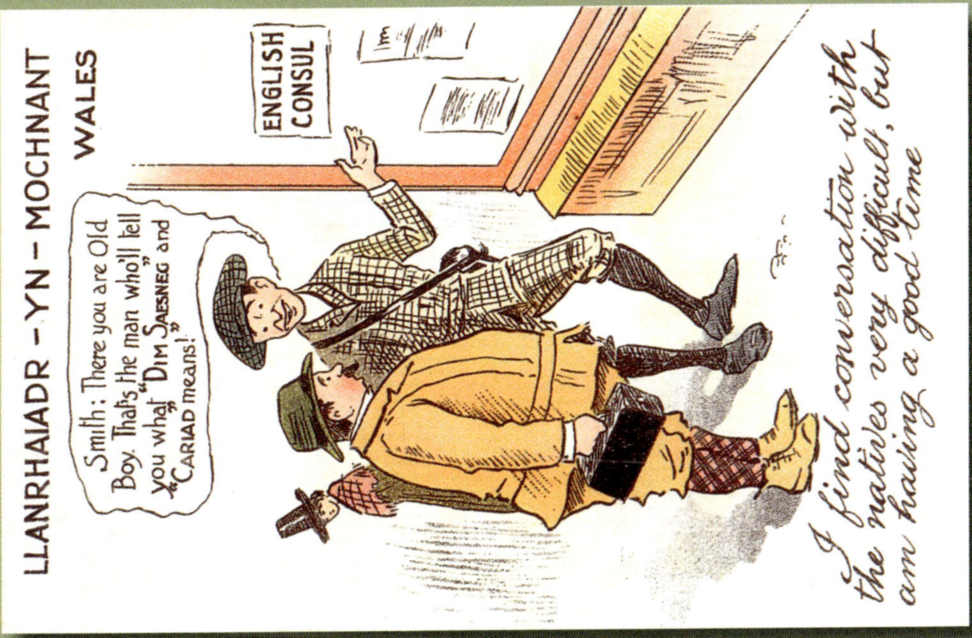

No. 2410

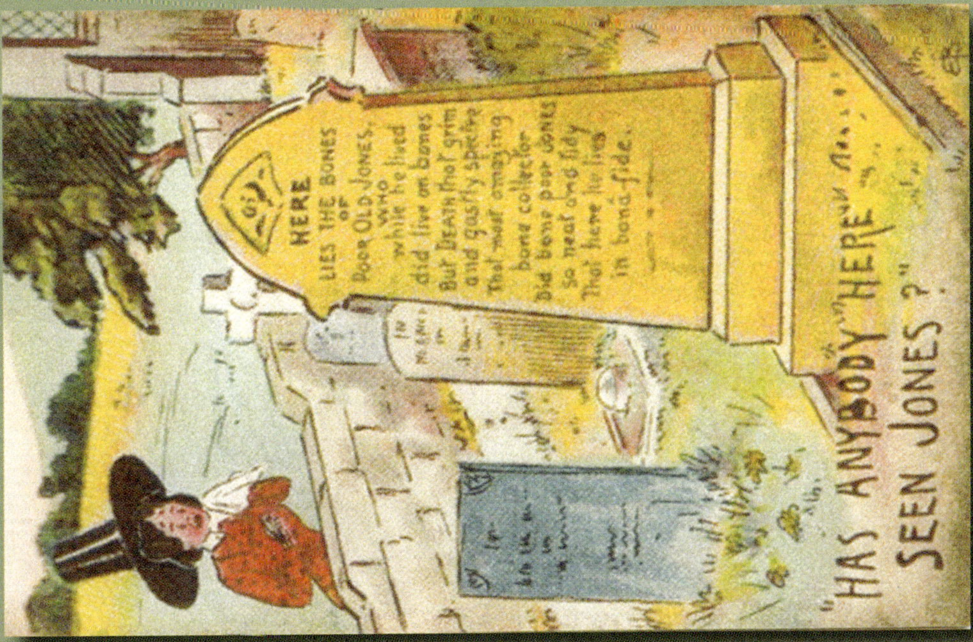

No. 456

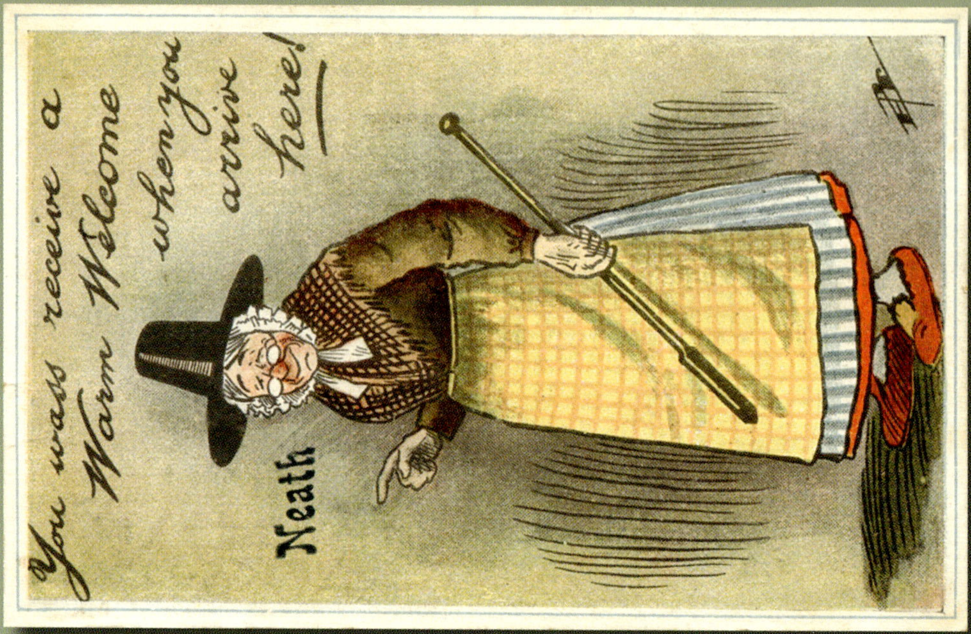
You wass receive a
Warm Welcome
when you
arrive
here!
Neath

No. 229

No. 206

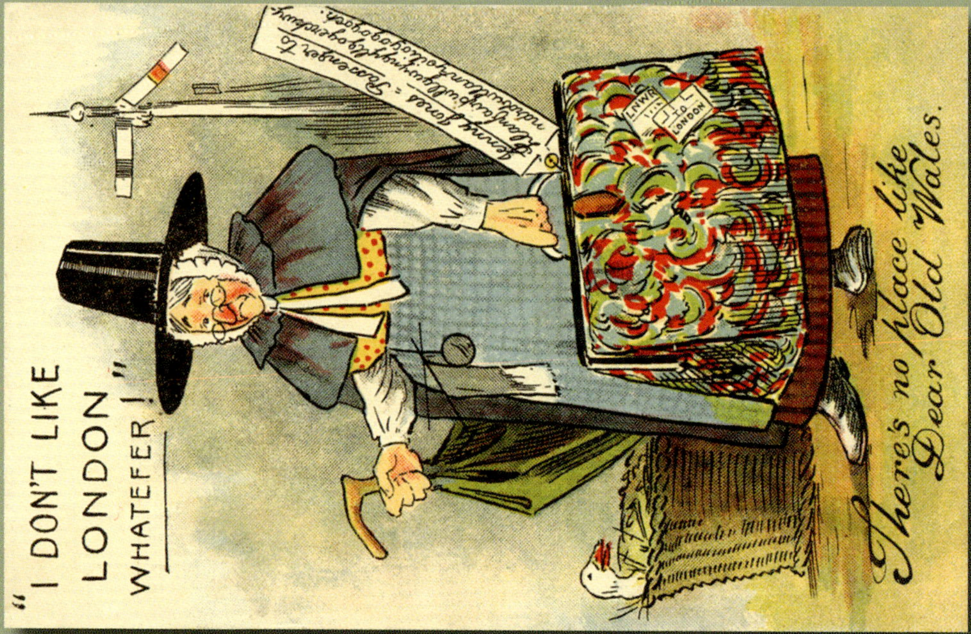
"I DON'T LIKE
LONDON
WHATEFER!"
There's no place like
Dear Old Wales.

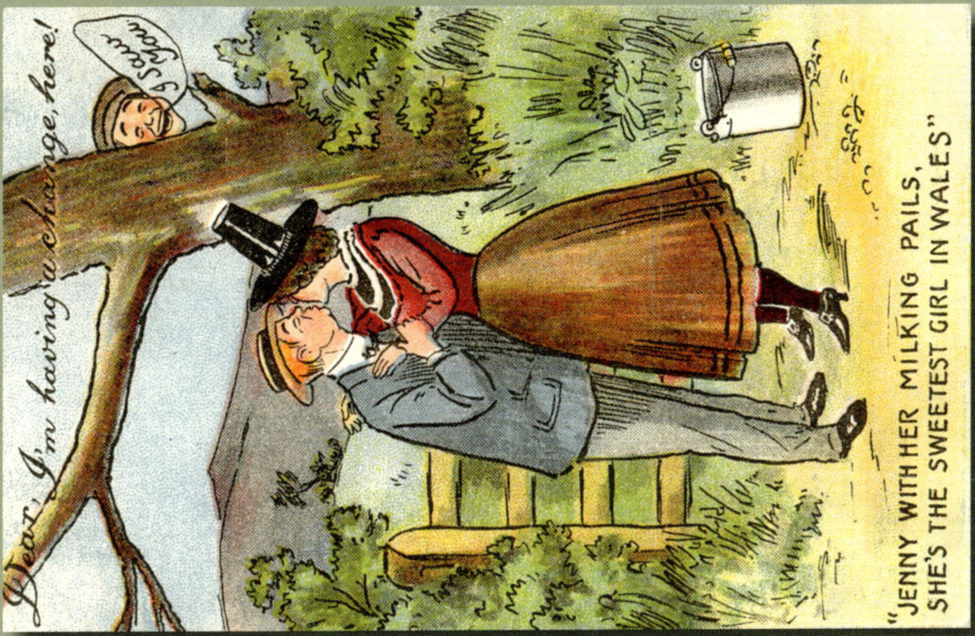

No. 207

No. 2604

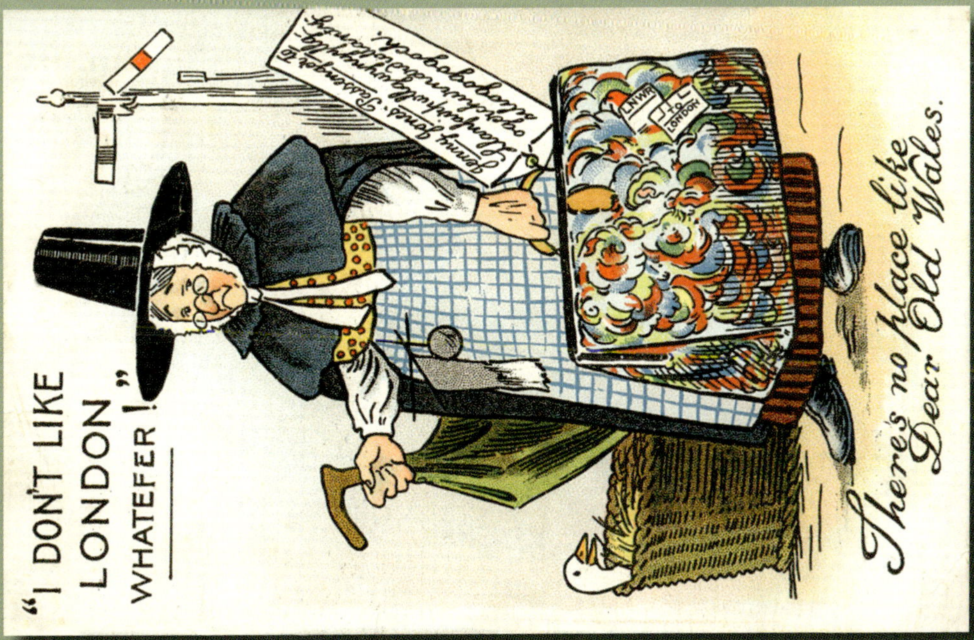

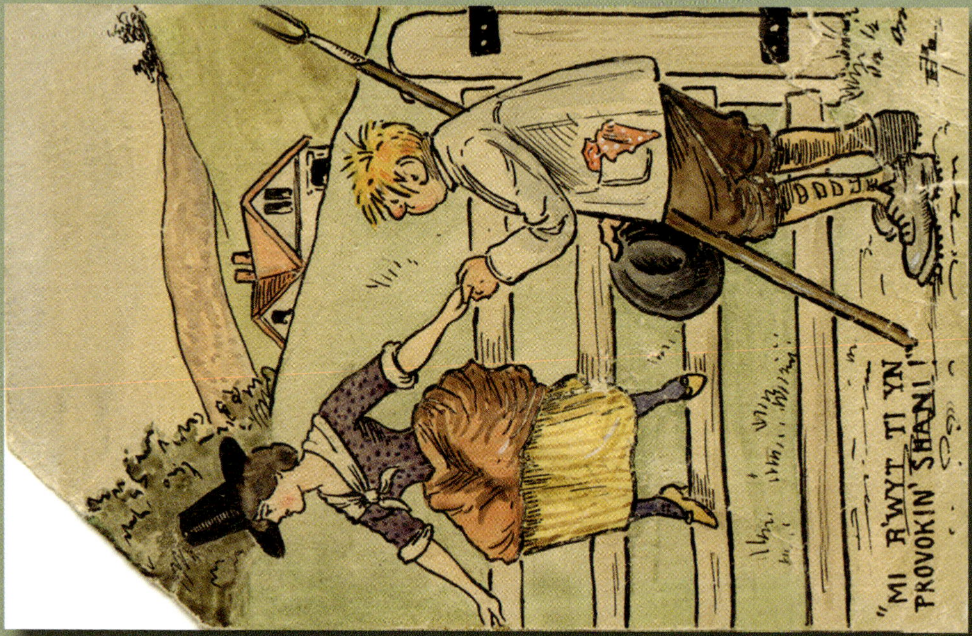

*N*o. *Not published*

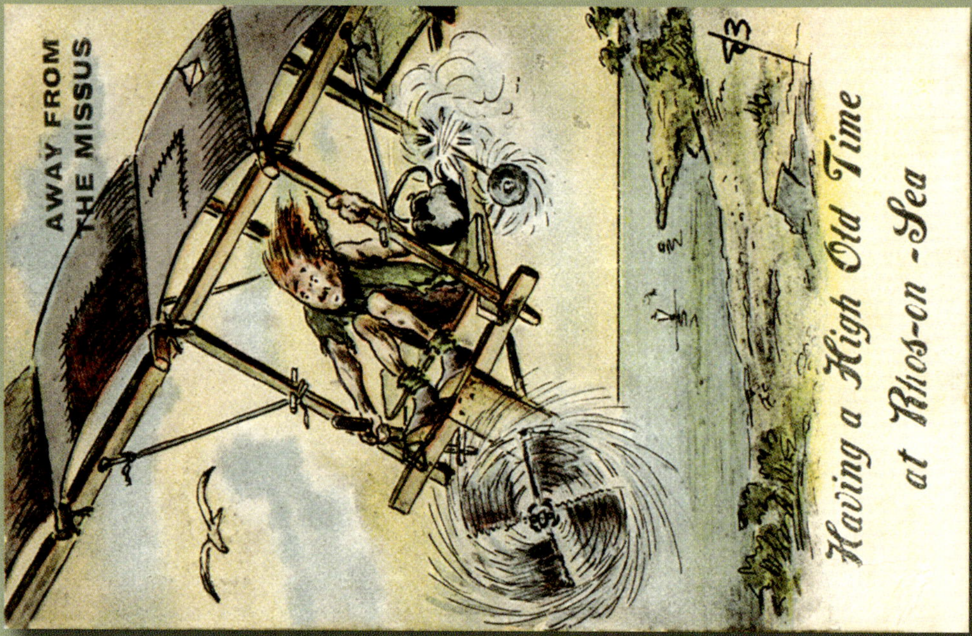

*N*o. *441*

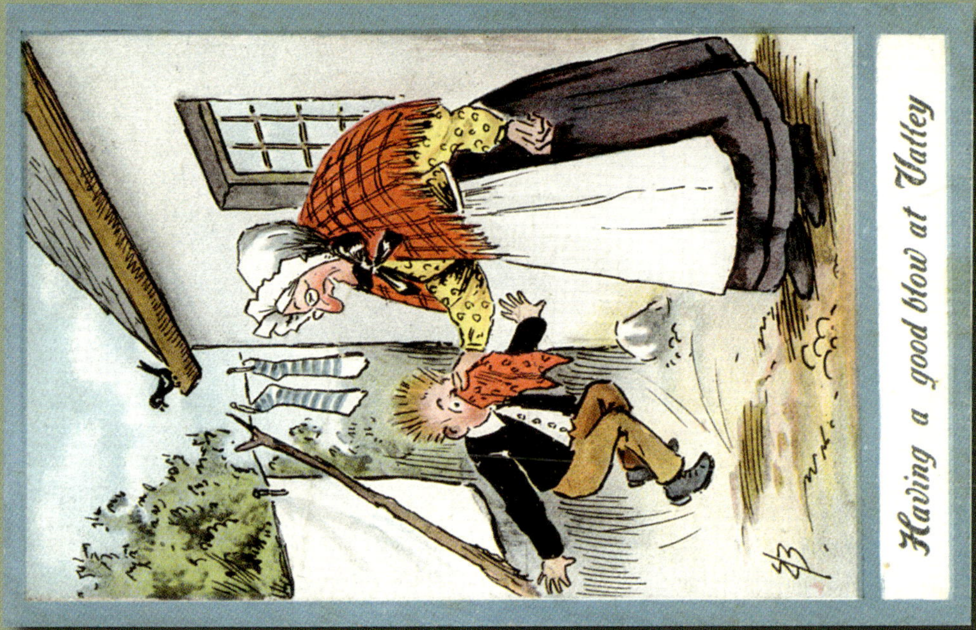
Having a good blow at Valley

Nº. 551

Nº. 226

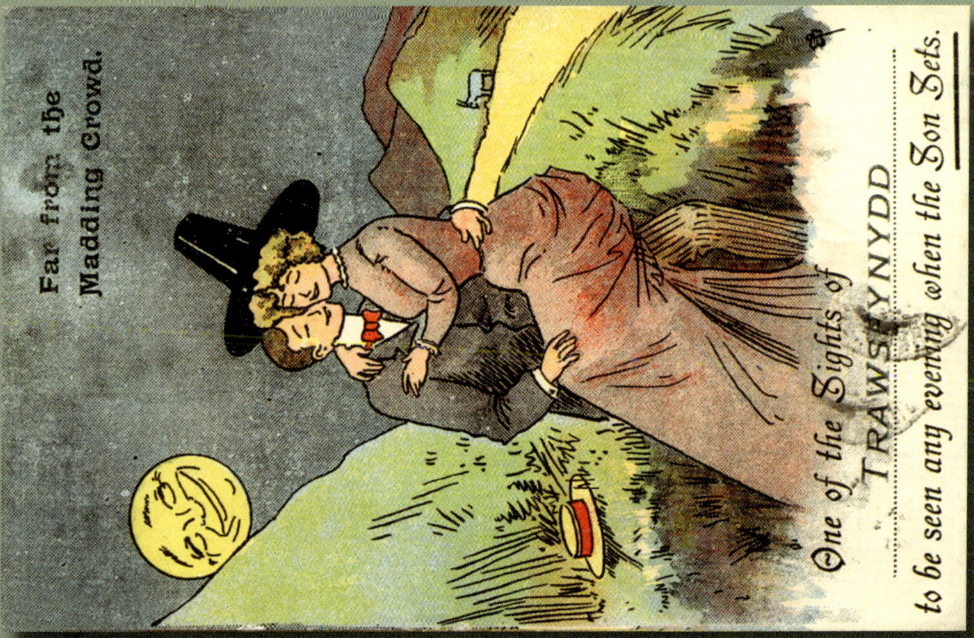
Far from the
Madding Crowd.
One of the Sights of
TRAWSFYNYDD
to be seen any evening when the Son Sets.

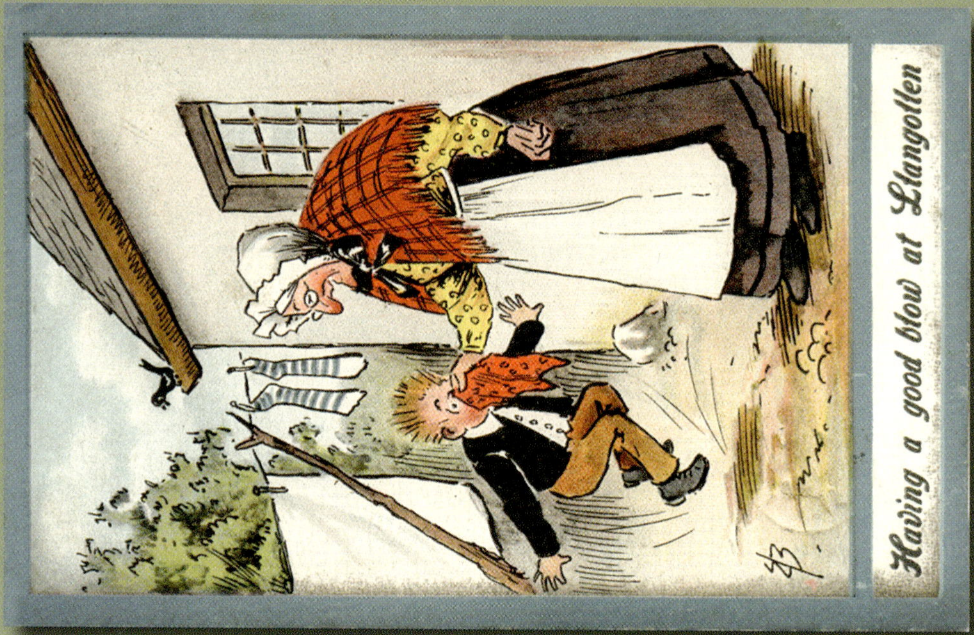
Having a good blow at Llangollen

No. 551

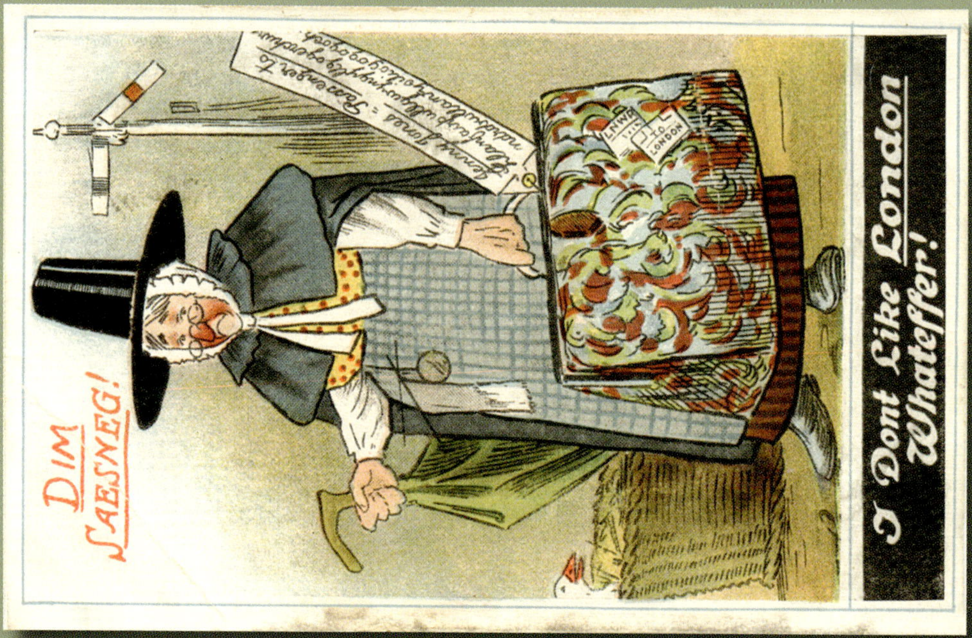
DIM SAESNEG!
I Dont Like London Whateffer!

No. 206

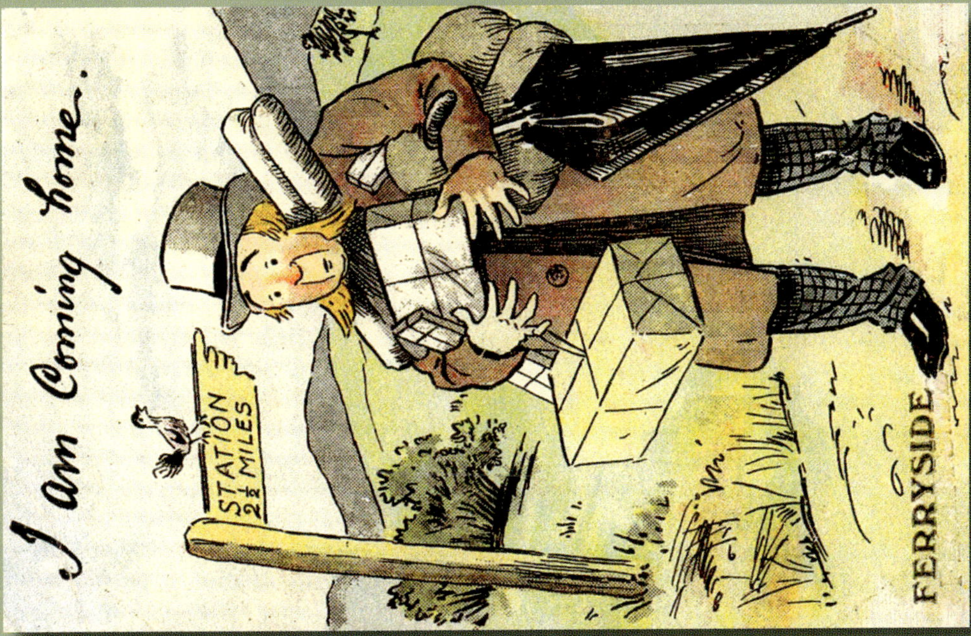
I am Coming home.
STATION 2½ MILES
FERRYSIDE

Nº. 216

Nº. 411

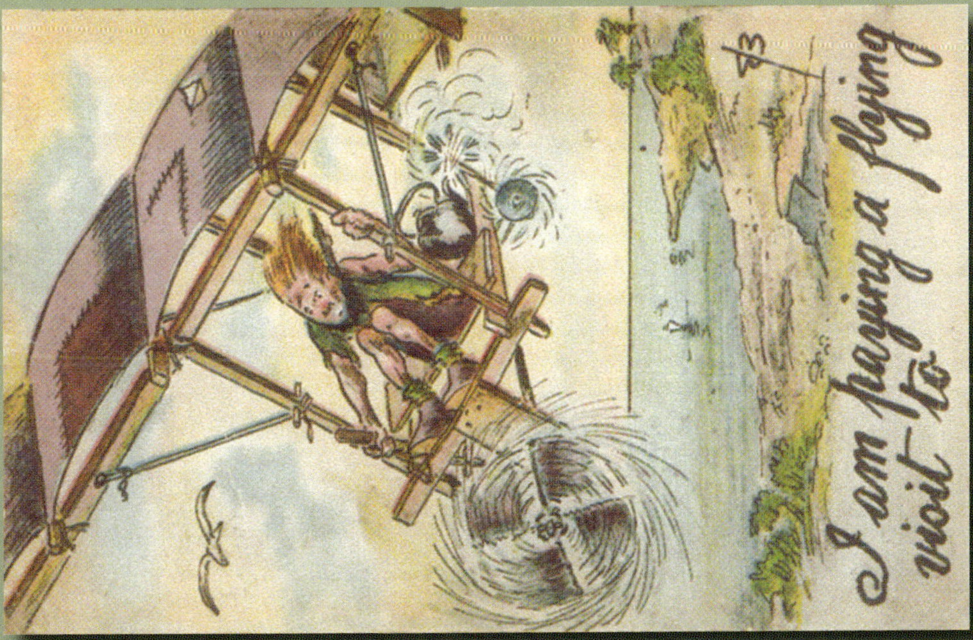
I am paying a flying visit to

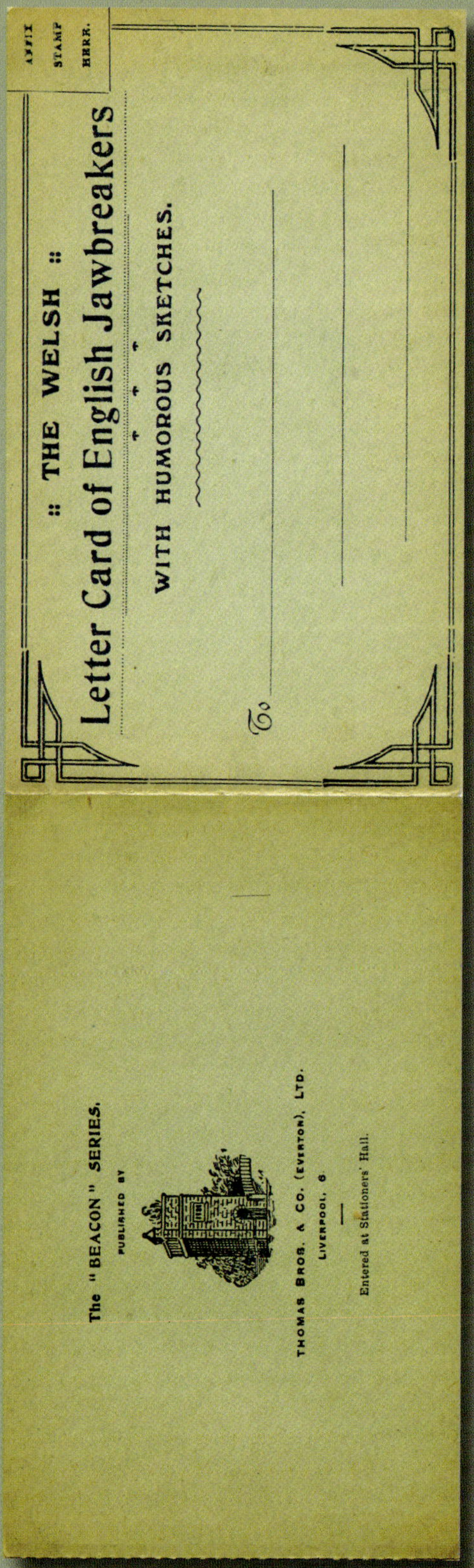
AFFIX STAMP HERE.
:: THE WELSH ::
Letter Card of English Jawbreakers
WITH HUMOROUS SKETCHES.
To
The "BEACON" SERIES.
PUBLISHED BY
THOMAS BROS. & CO. (EVERTON), LTD.
LIVERPOOL, 6.
Entered at Stationers' Hall.

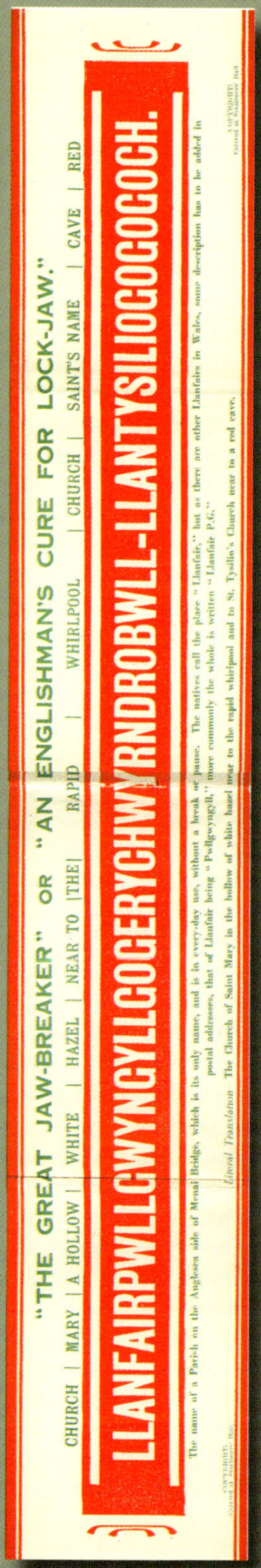
"THE GREAT JAW-BREAKER" OR "AN ENGLISHMAN'S CURE FOR LOCK-JAW."
CHURCH | MARY | A HOLLOW | WHITE | HAZEL | NEAR TO | THE | RAPID | WHIRLPOOL | CHURCH | SAINT'S NAME | CAVE | RED
LLANFAIRPWLLGWYNGYLLGOGERYCHWYRNDROBWLL-LLANTYSILIOGOGOGOCH.
The name of a Parish on the Anglesea side of Menai Bridge, which is its only name, and is in every-day use, without a break or pause. The natives call the place "Llanfair," but as there are other Llanfairs in Wales, some description has to be added in postal addresses, that of Llanfair being "Pwllgwyngyll," more commonly the whole is written "Llanfair P.G."
Literal Translation The Church of Saint Mary in the hollow of white hazel near to the rapid whirlpool and to St. Tysilio's Church near to a red cave.

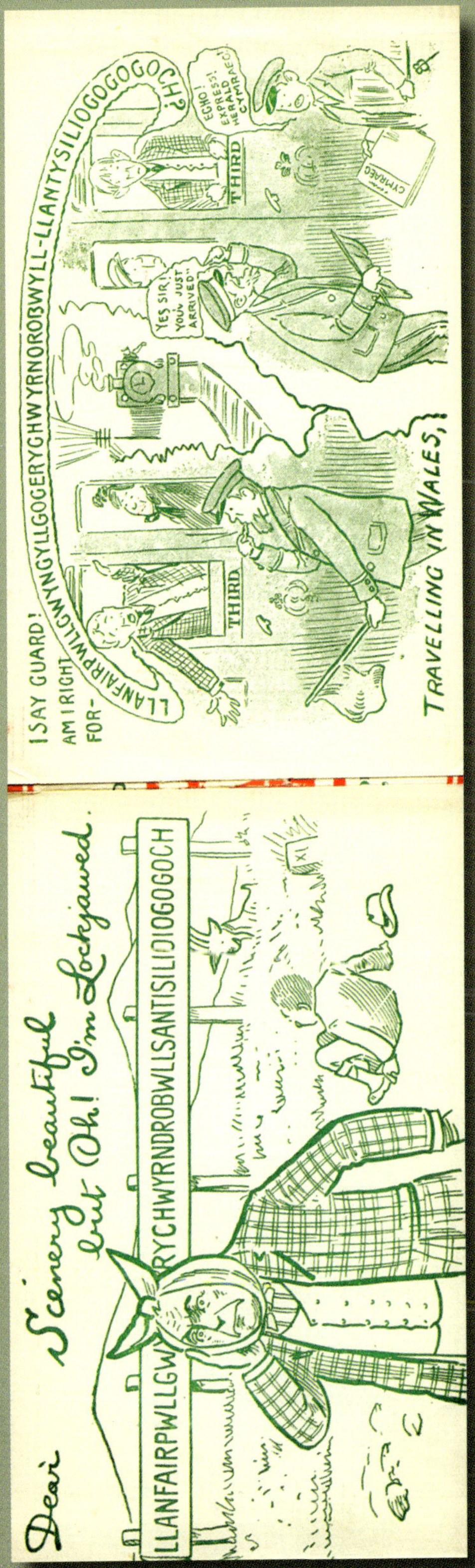

Facing and above: The Welsh Lettercard of English Jawbreakers

The Paintings and Drawings of Ernest Burrows

The following pages show some of the paintings and drawings produced by Ernest Burrows. Most are of local scenes in and around Llangollen as well as some unidentified places which he may have visited or copied from books or magazines. There are also drawings taken from one of the many sketchbooks that he filled during his lifetime. He was always sketching local characters and buildings around the town, in case they would become useful material for his postcards and illustrations. The photograph of Ernest's watercolour paintbox shows just how he left it over ninety years ago, preserved and kept by the family as a memento of a very special and talented man.

The first illustration shows a card painted by Ernest that was never published – possibly painted for the amusement of himself and local acquaintances in Llangollen, featuring local characters and their nicknames and revolving around a character named Cheina Tom.

The Cheina Tom story started in the early 1900s when a wild, feral cat nicknamed by Llangollen locals as 'Cheina Tom' terrorised the town. Tom was a

The unpublished 'Cheina Tom' card.

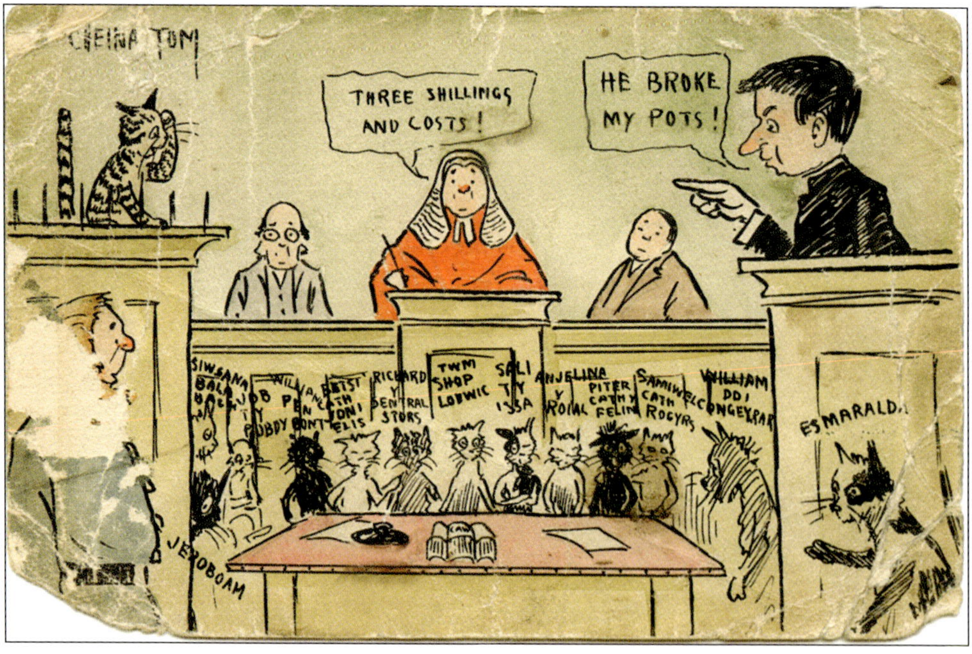

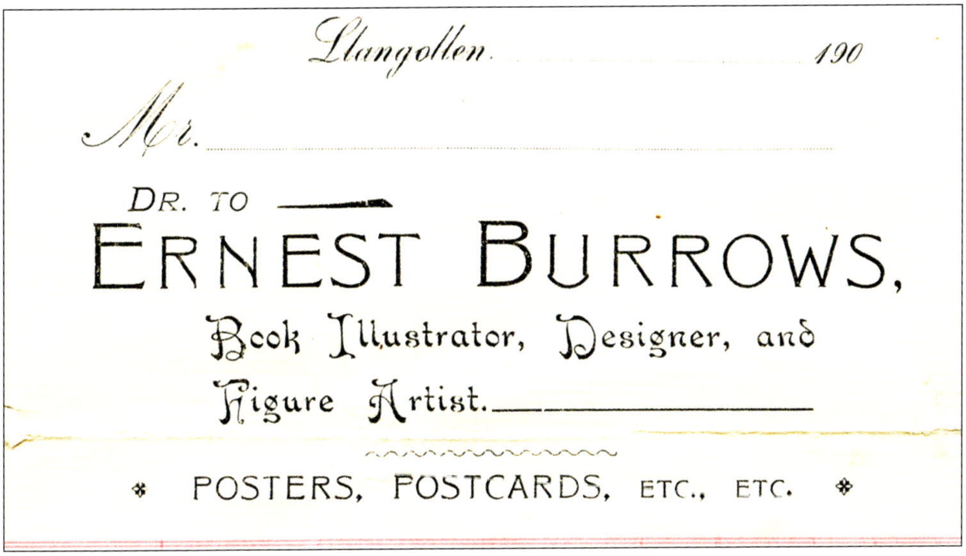

Llangollen 190

Mr.

DR. TO

ERNEST BURROWS,

Book Illustrator, Designer, and Figure Artist.

POSTERS, POSTCARDS, ETC., ETC.

Ernest's letterhead.

dreadful cat! He would steal food from the shops in the town and sneak into people's houses breaking pots and dishes and causing all manner of damage. Nobody was spared, houses, churches, farms, shops, all had cause to complain. Ernest painted this humorous postcard depicting the trial of Cheina Tom for all his misdemeanours. He set the scene in the local court where Cheina Tom appeared to be put on trial in front of a judge. He featured Cheina Tom in the dock with all the local shopkeepers as cats, including Siwsana Bala Bach, Job Ty Popty, Wilph Pen Bont, Richard Sentral Stores, Twm Shop Lodwic, Sali Ty Issa, Anjelina Y Royal, Piter Cath Y Felin, Samiwel Cath Rogyrs, William Ddi Comgeryrar and Esmaralda. The postcard also shows the local Llangollen policeman of that time, Jeroboam.

A major part of Ernest's income came from signwriting and amongst his papers is a large bound book containing numerous examples of the illuminated lettering which he designed and

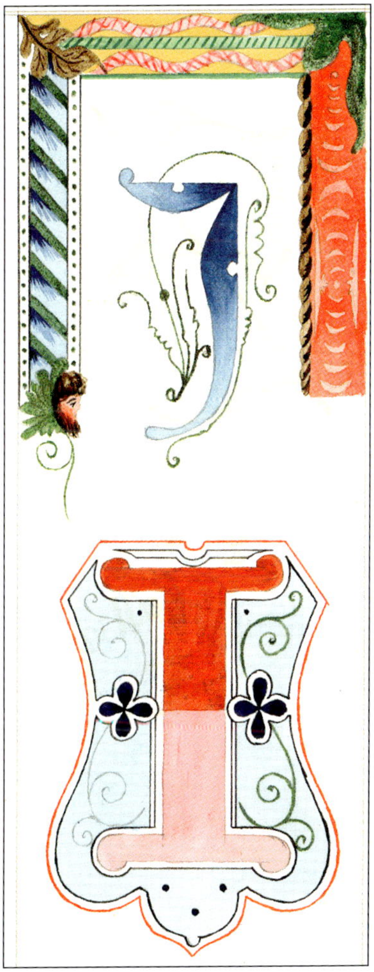

Two samples of Ernest's illuminated letters.

utilised in his business. These and the drawings in his sketchbooks clearly show the high quality of his draghtsmanship, all the more remarkable when one considers that he appears to have had no formal training in any aspect of art.

Below and facing, further examples of Ernest's illuminated letters.

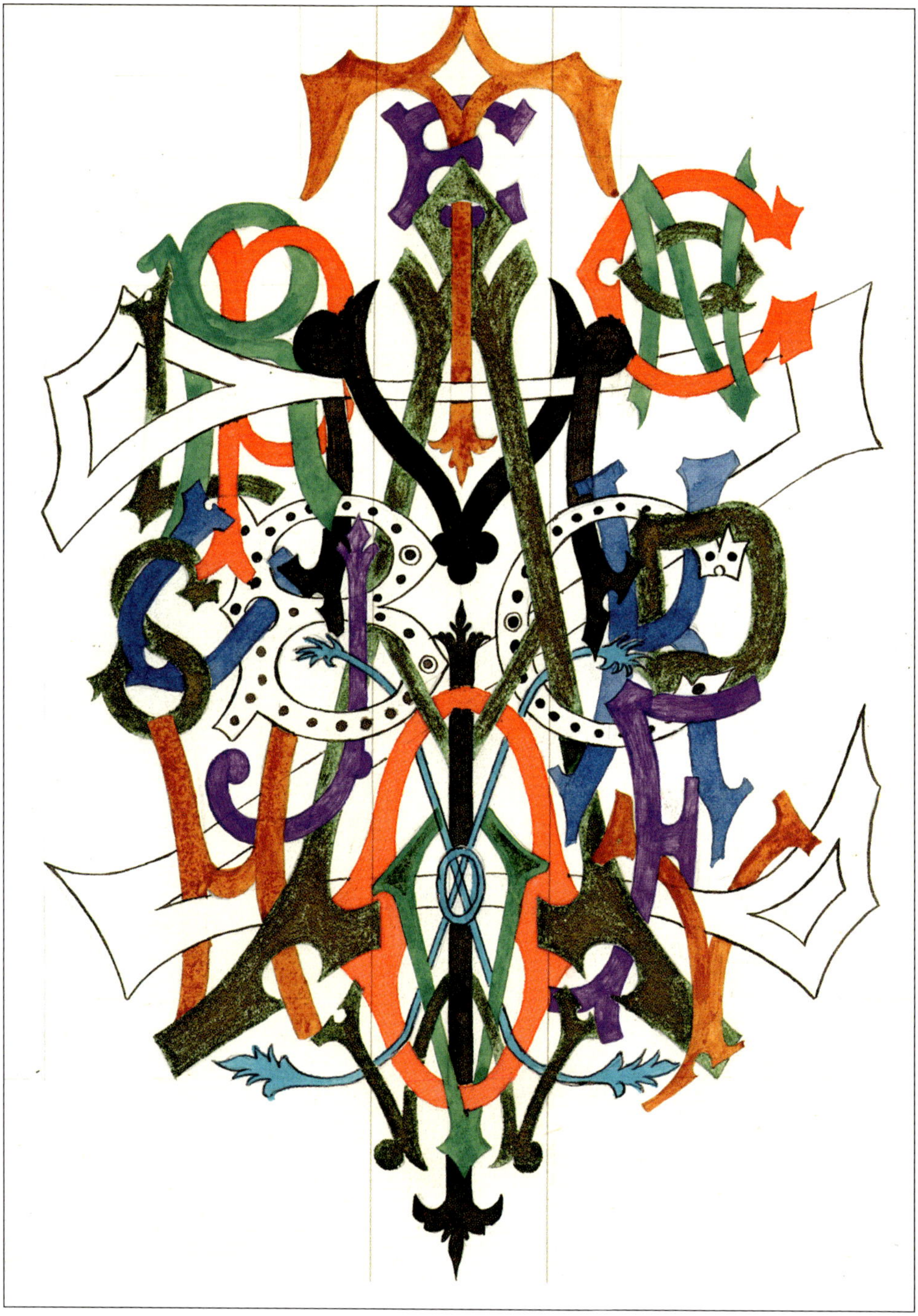

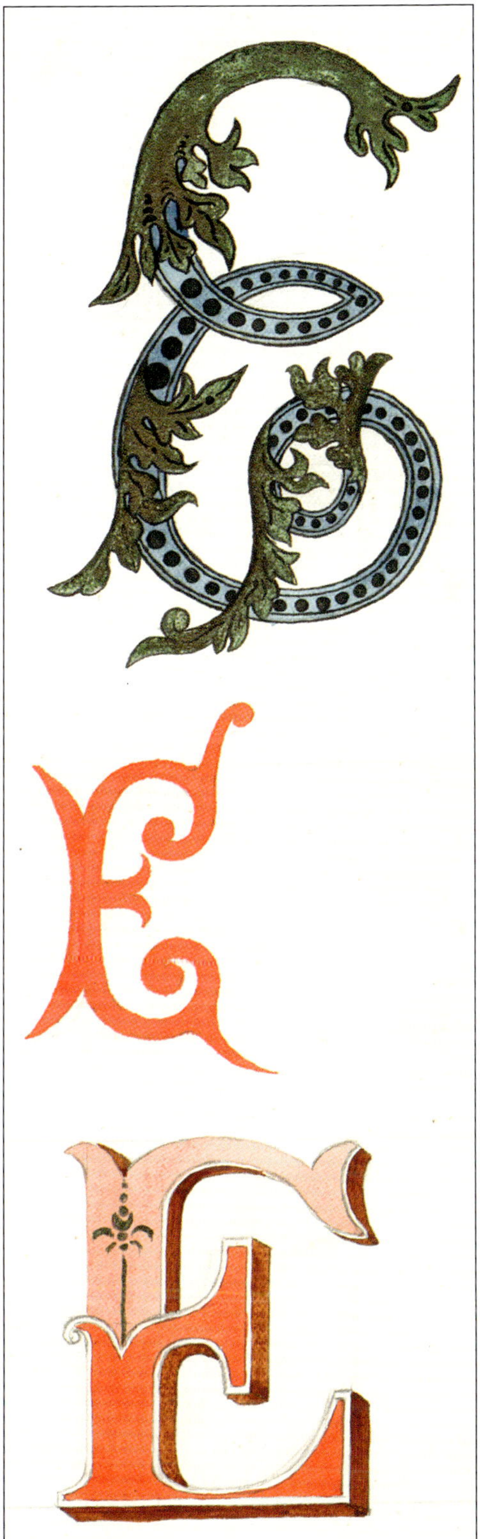

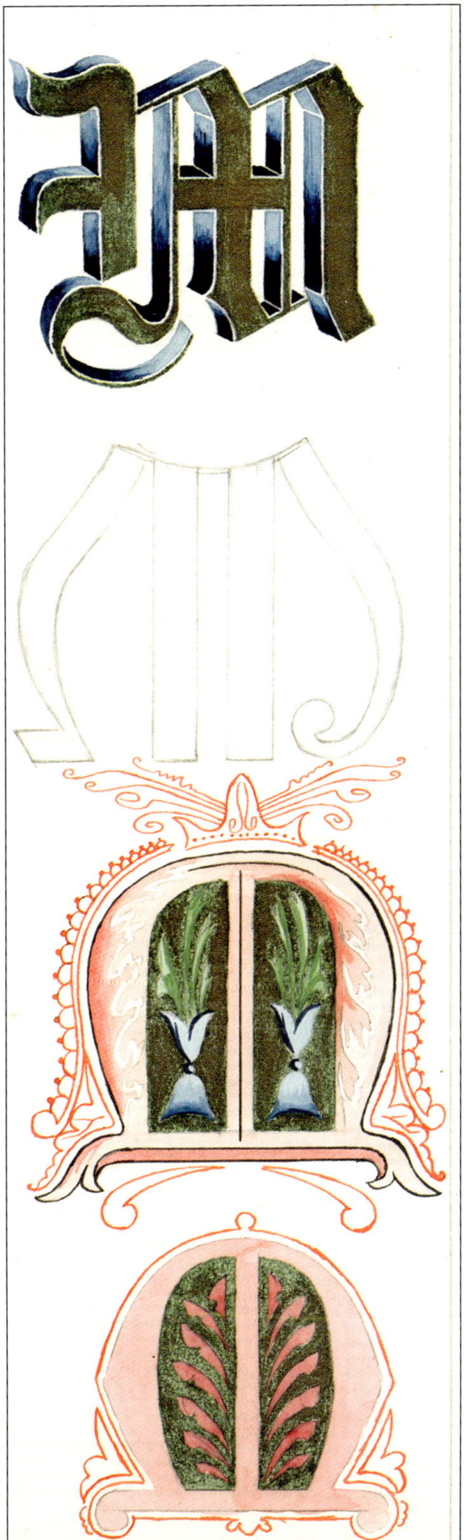

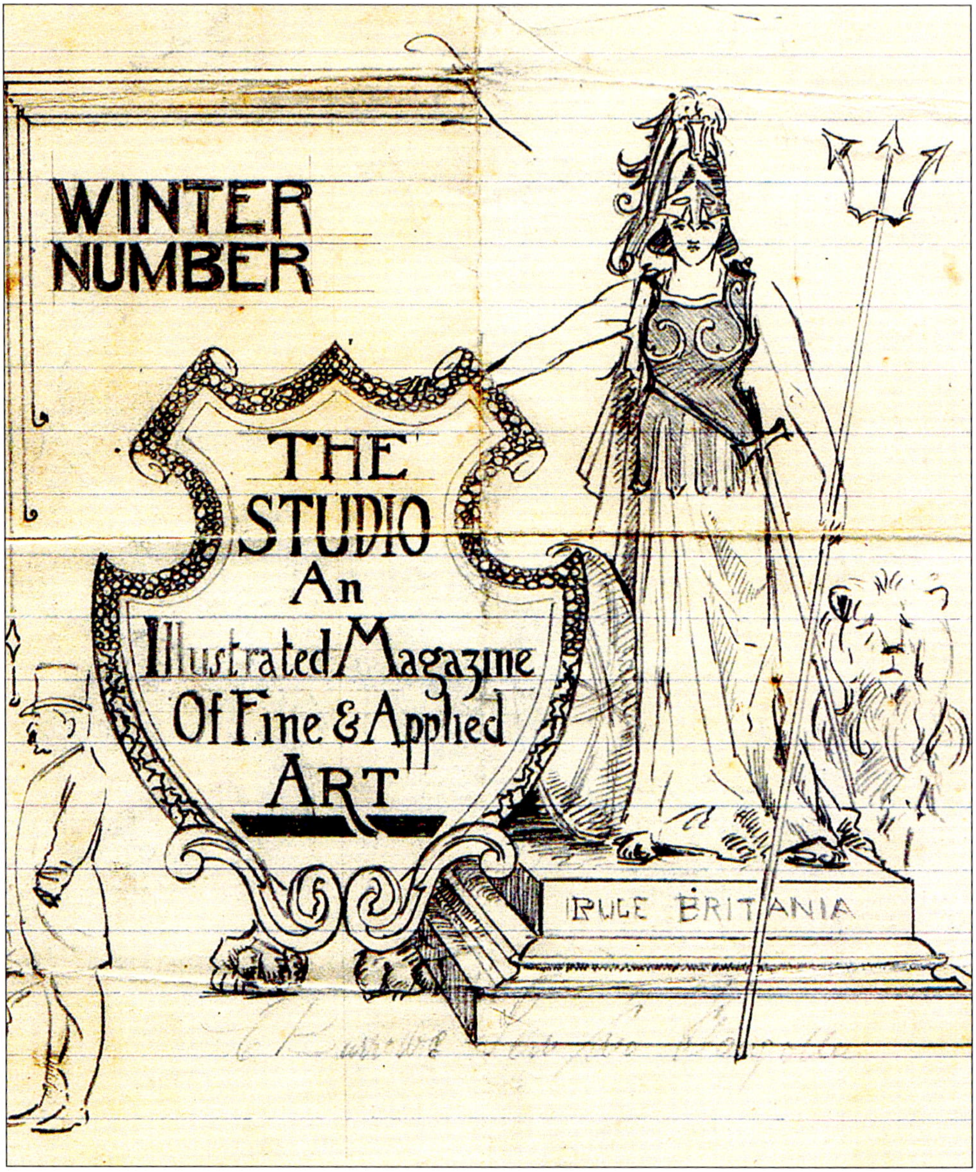

Cover design for the winter issue of The Studio *a pretigious illustrated magazine first published in April 1893, becoming one of the most successful fine-art publications. It featured the work of many notable artists and designers including Aubrey Beardsley and Charles Rennie Mackintosh. Whether this design was ever actually adopted by the magazine is unrecorded. It is still published today under the title* Studio International.

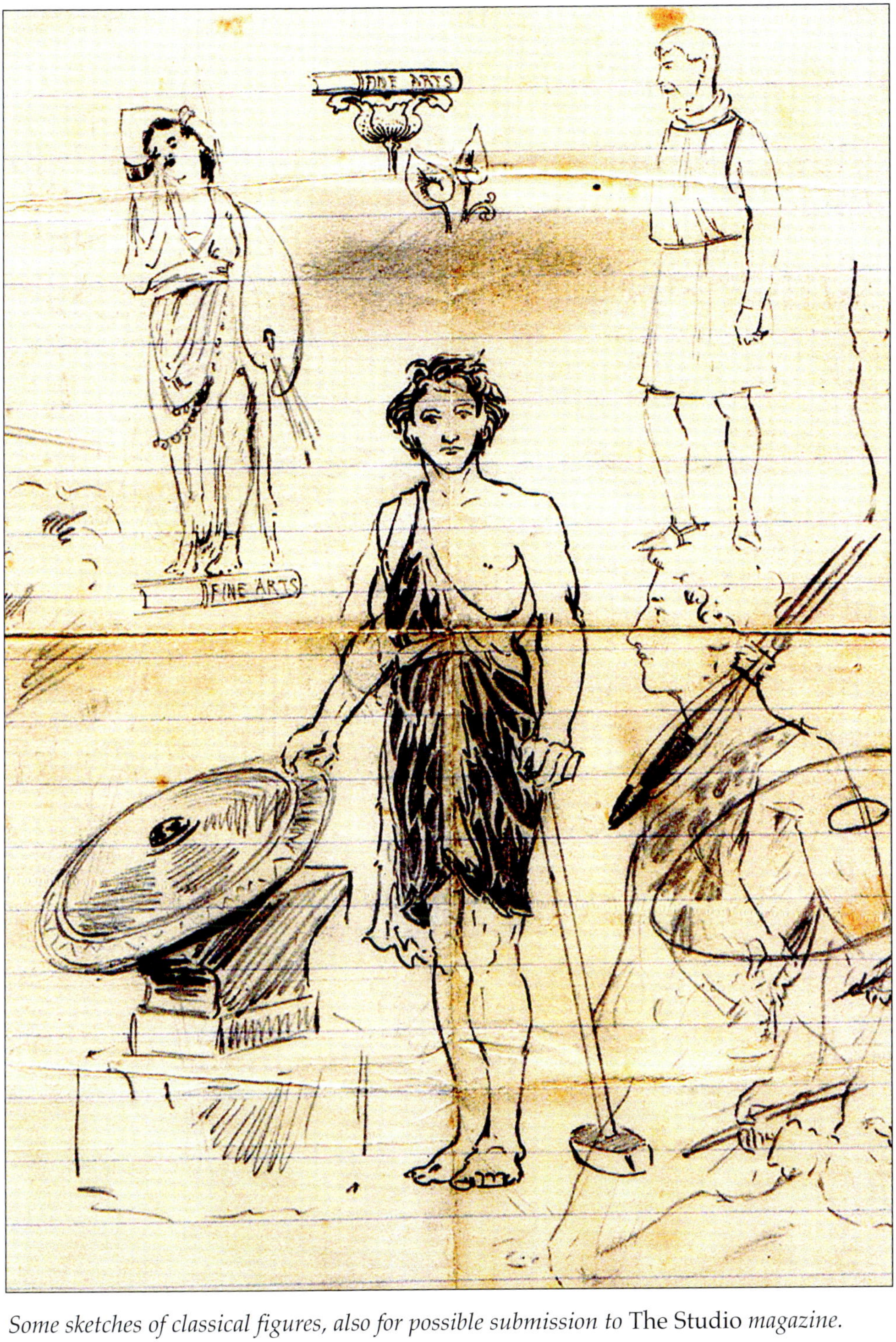

Some sketches of classical figures, also for possible submission to The Studio *magazine.*

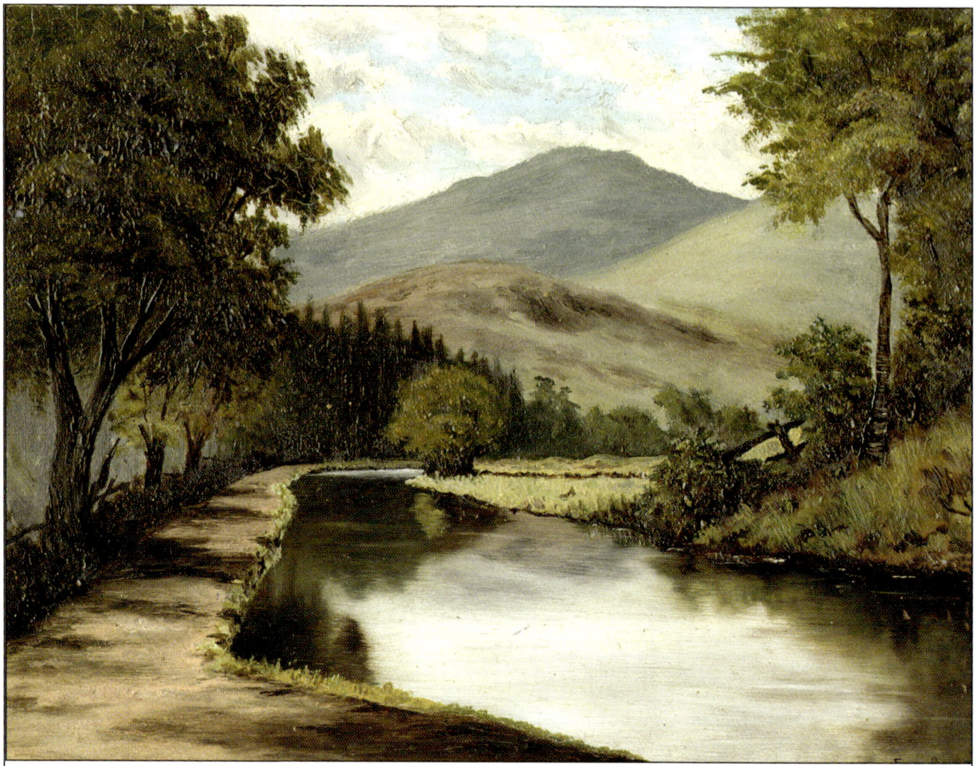

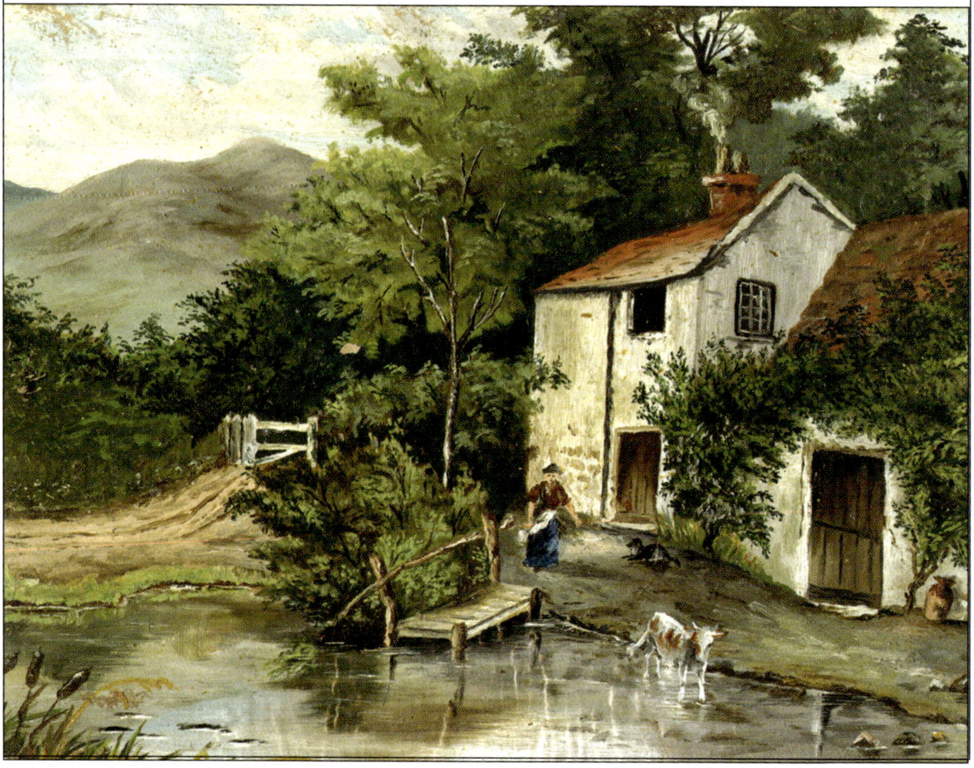

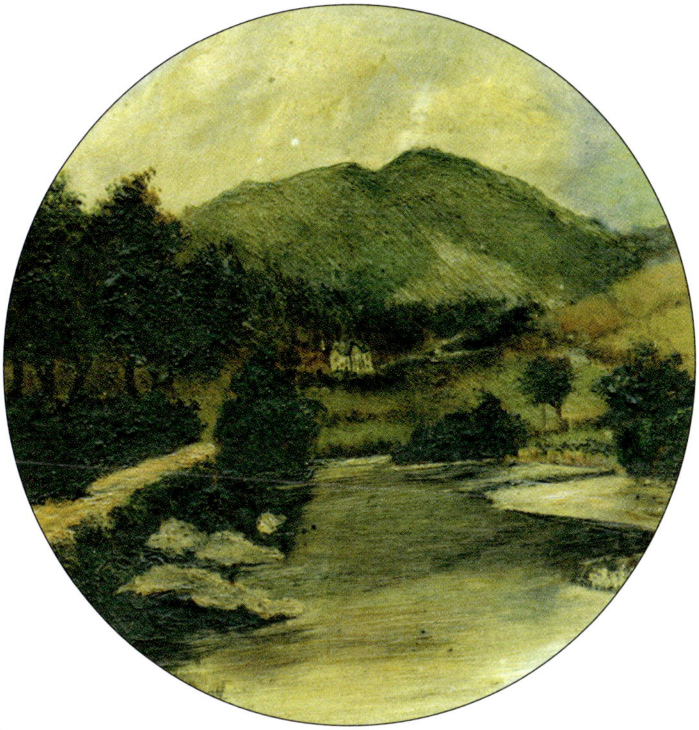

Facing & above: Some examples of Ernest Burrow's oil paintings, produced on a wooden base which has now become subjected to water damage. All undated.

Below: Ernest Burrows' watercolour paint box.

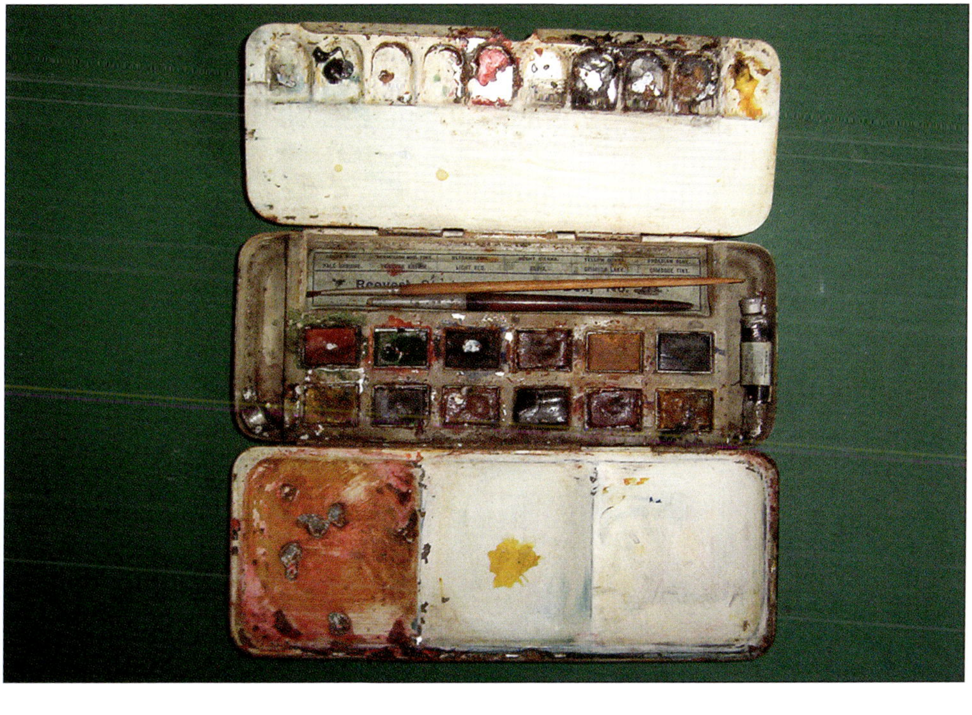

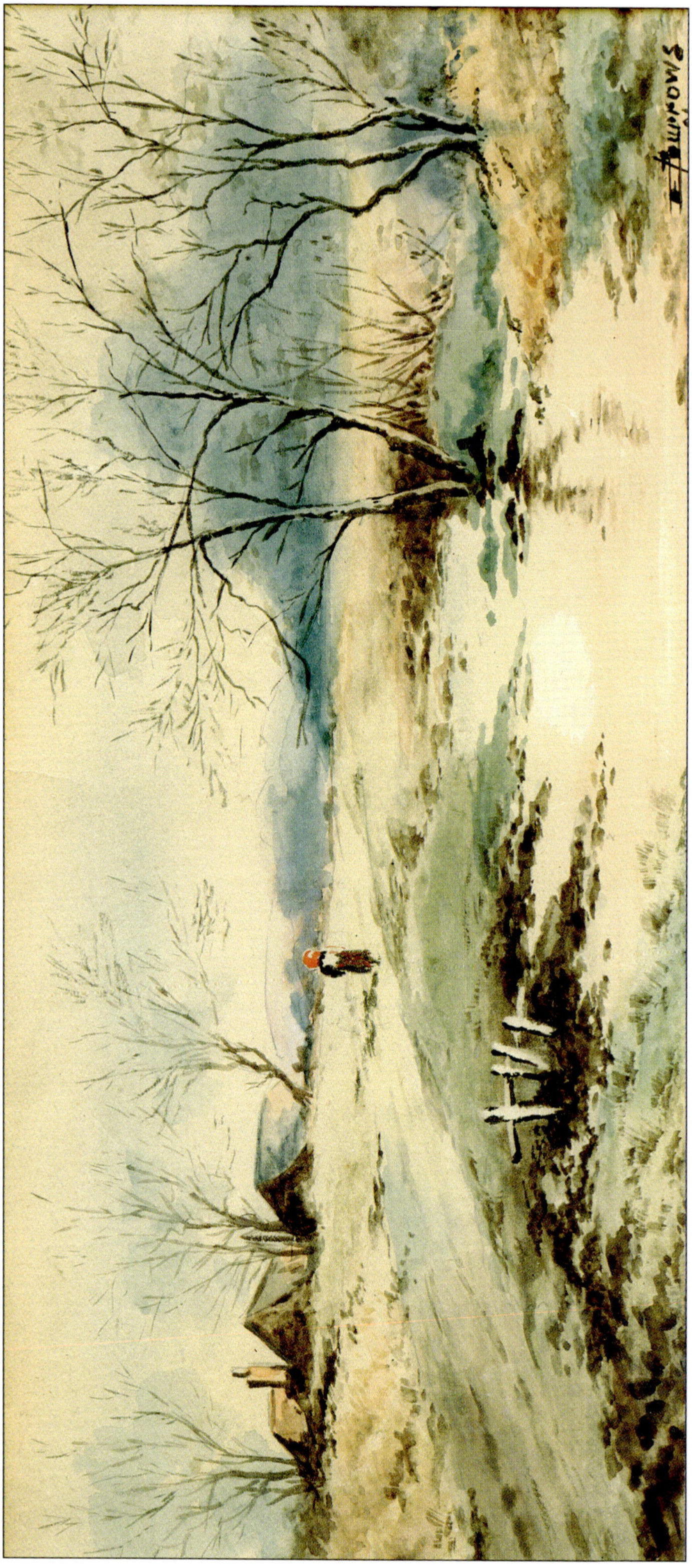

A watercolour landscape painted in 1901.

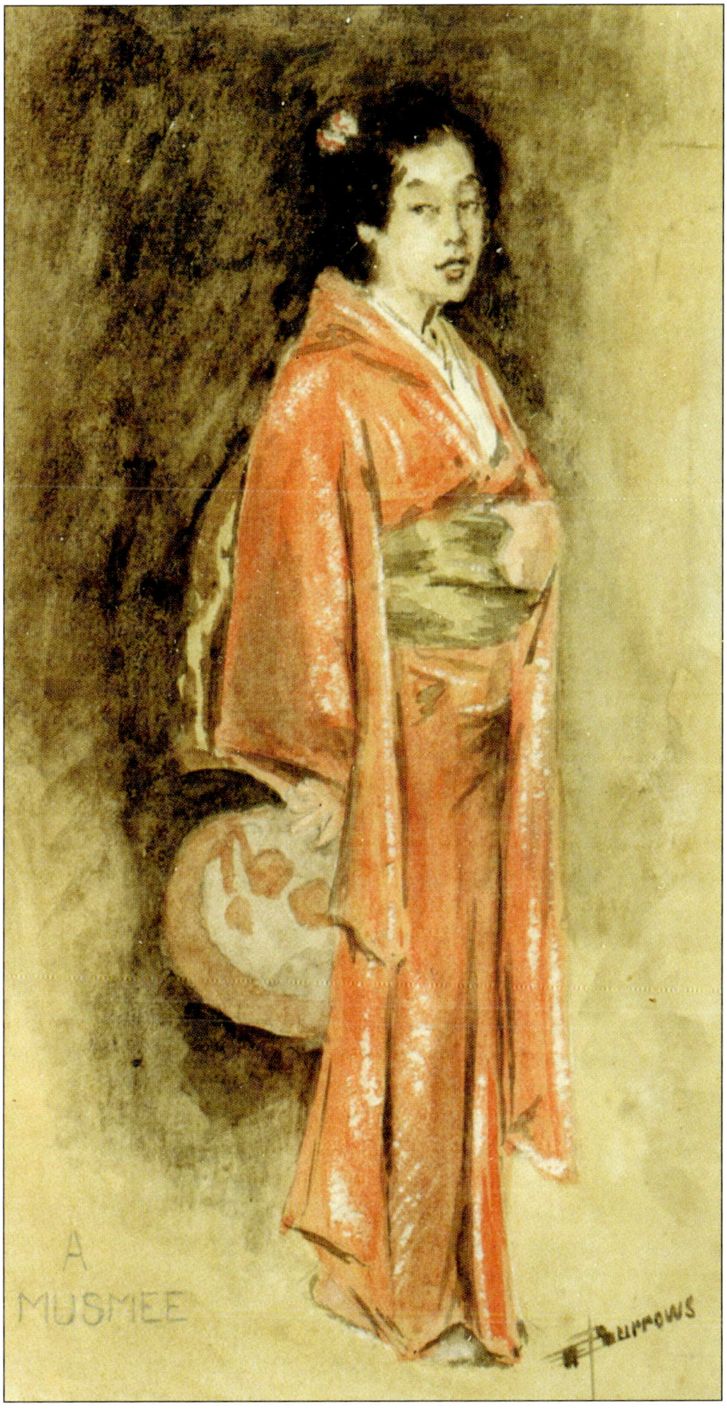

Watercolour of a Japanese Musmee, date unknown.

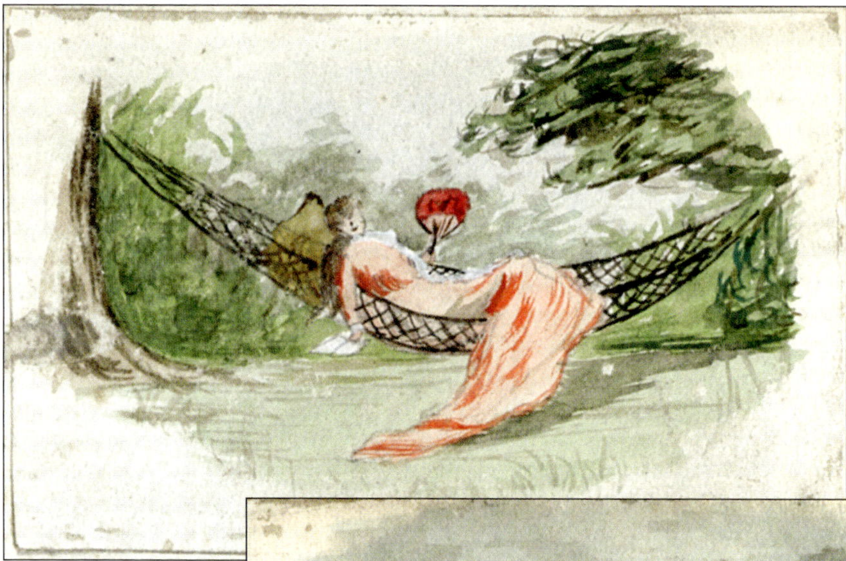

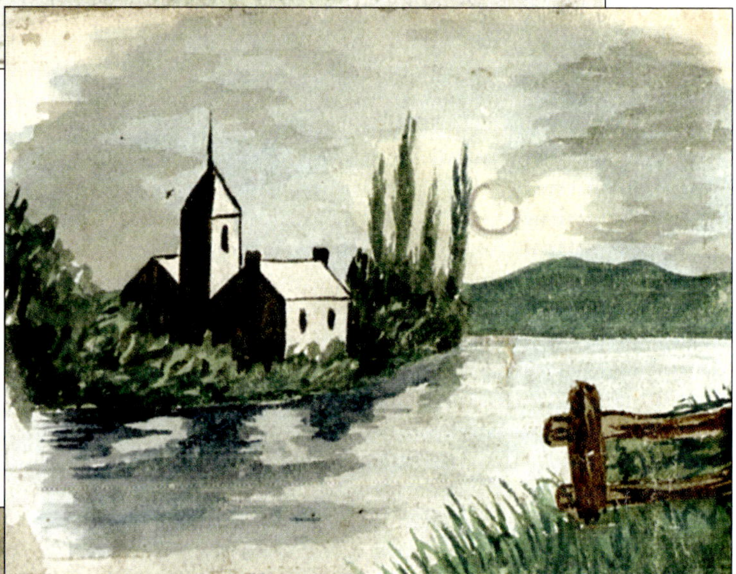

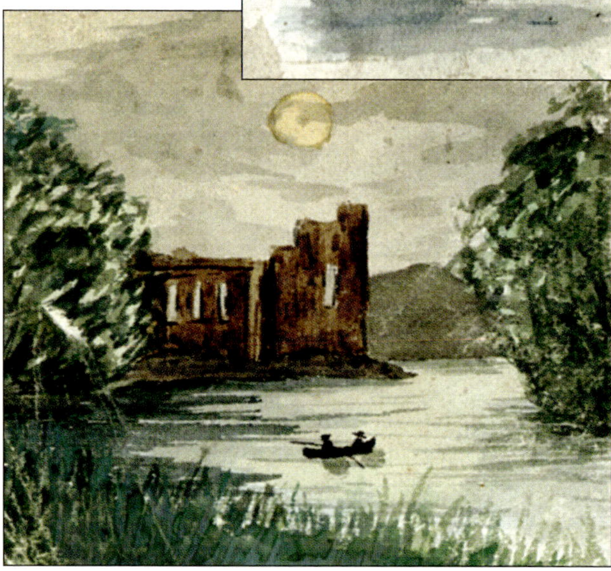

Three miniature waterclour sketches. Undated.

Facing: Pen and ink drawing, 1896.

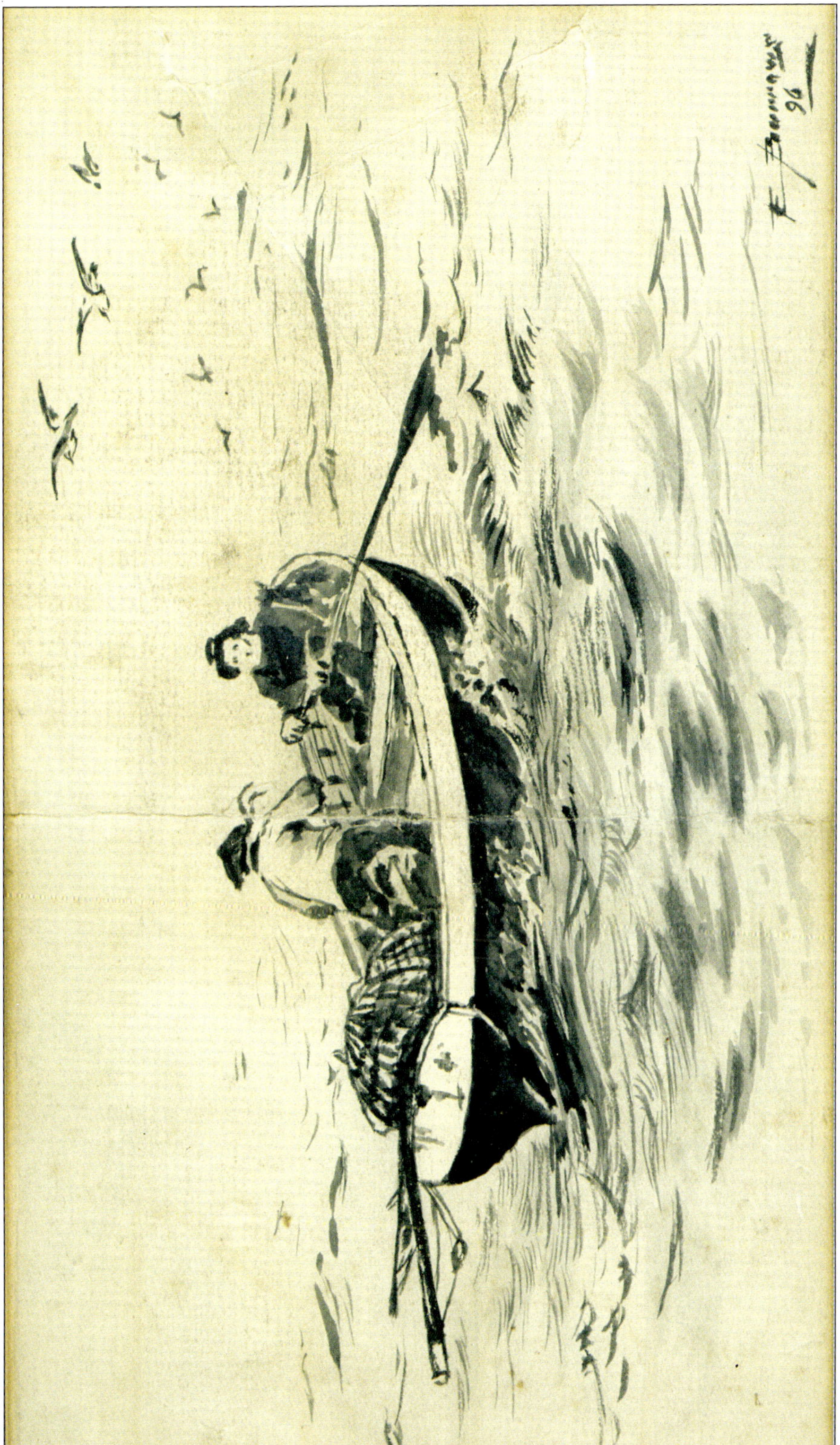

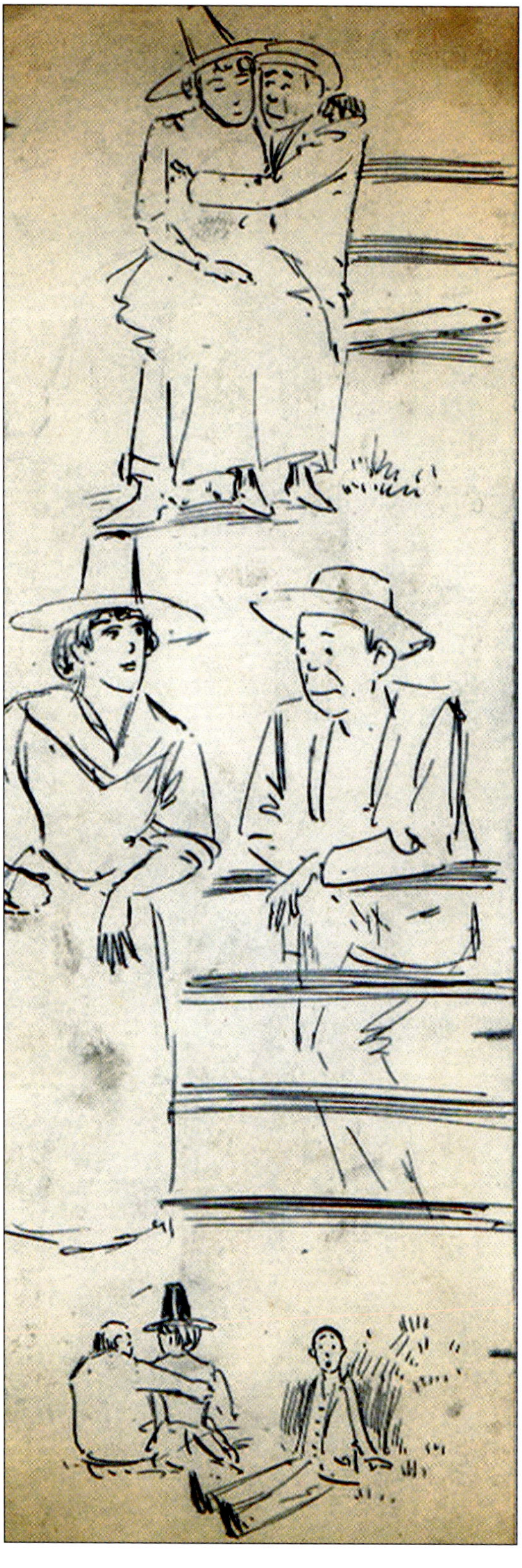

Ernest Burrows had a number of sketch books which covered much of his working career. Unfortunately, only one complete book (which dates for the mid 1890s) has survived, along with a number of unbound rough sketches for postcards.

Left and facing top:
A series of preliminary sketches for the Everton Series postcards illustrating various studies for courting couples, including the trademark Welsh Lady figure.

Facing centre: A series of sketches showing the development of the facial expression of one of his postcard characters. The upside-down handwriting reads: 'Said she "I'd say, yes, but I'm shy." But she kicked him and sent him sky-high.' which would suggest that he worked on the drawing and the caption/joke at the same time and recorded both in his sketch book.

Facing bottom: Most of Ernest Burrows' cartoon cards and illustrations were placed in a background setting which he based on real locations. Scattered throughout the book are sketches of potential backgrounds executed whilst on his walks in the Llangollen area.

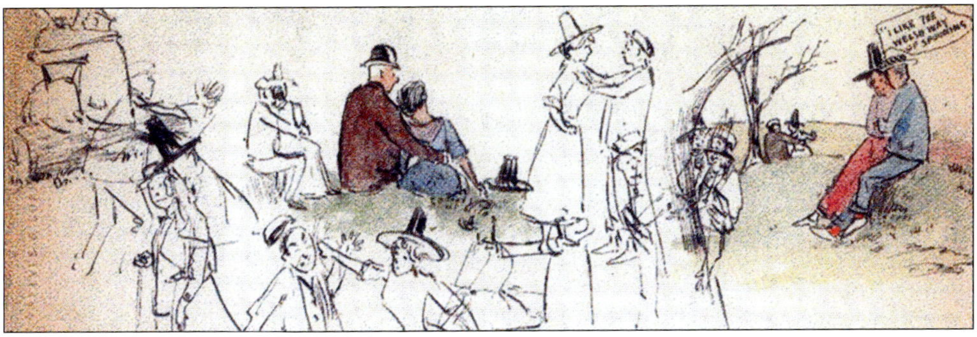
"I LIKE THE WELSH WAY OF SPOONING

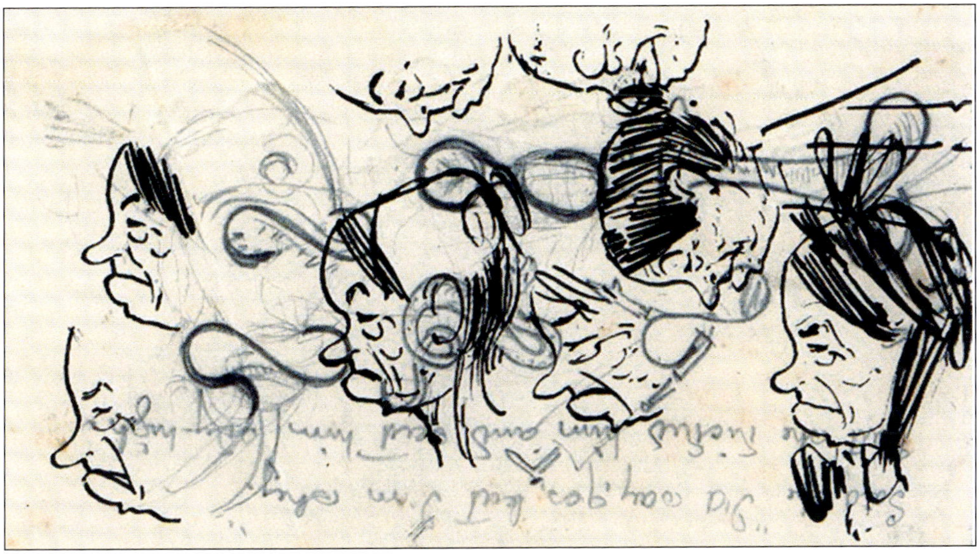

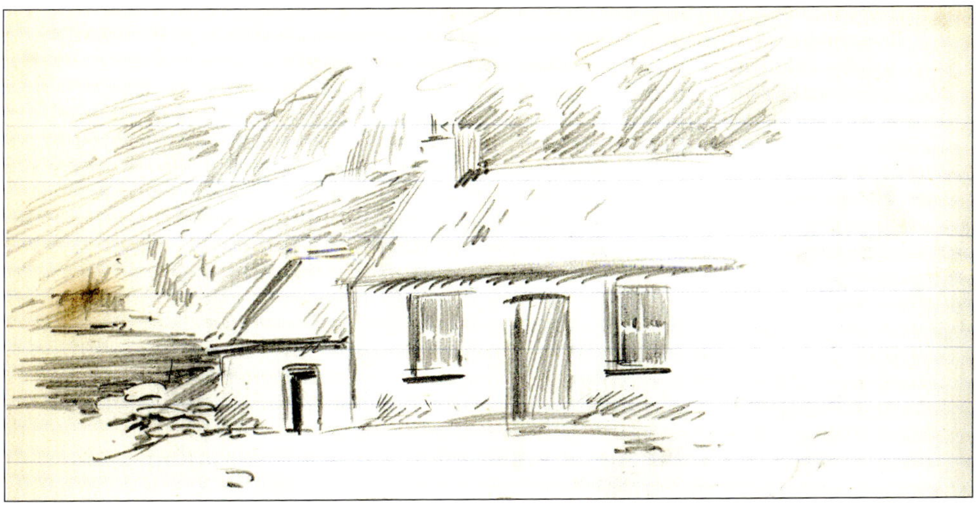

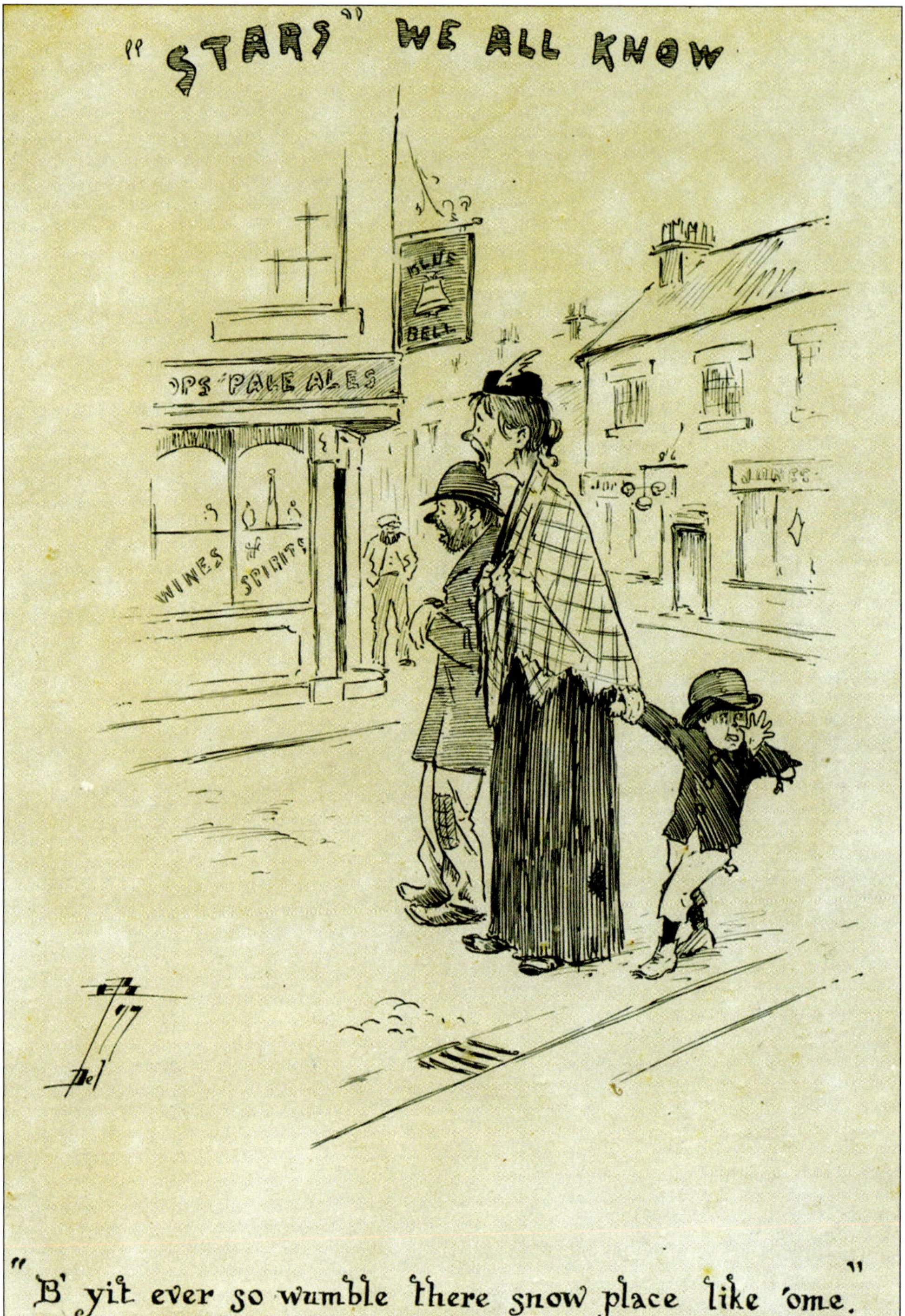

A traditional cartoon that makes an important social comment on life in the 1890s.

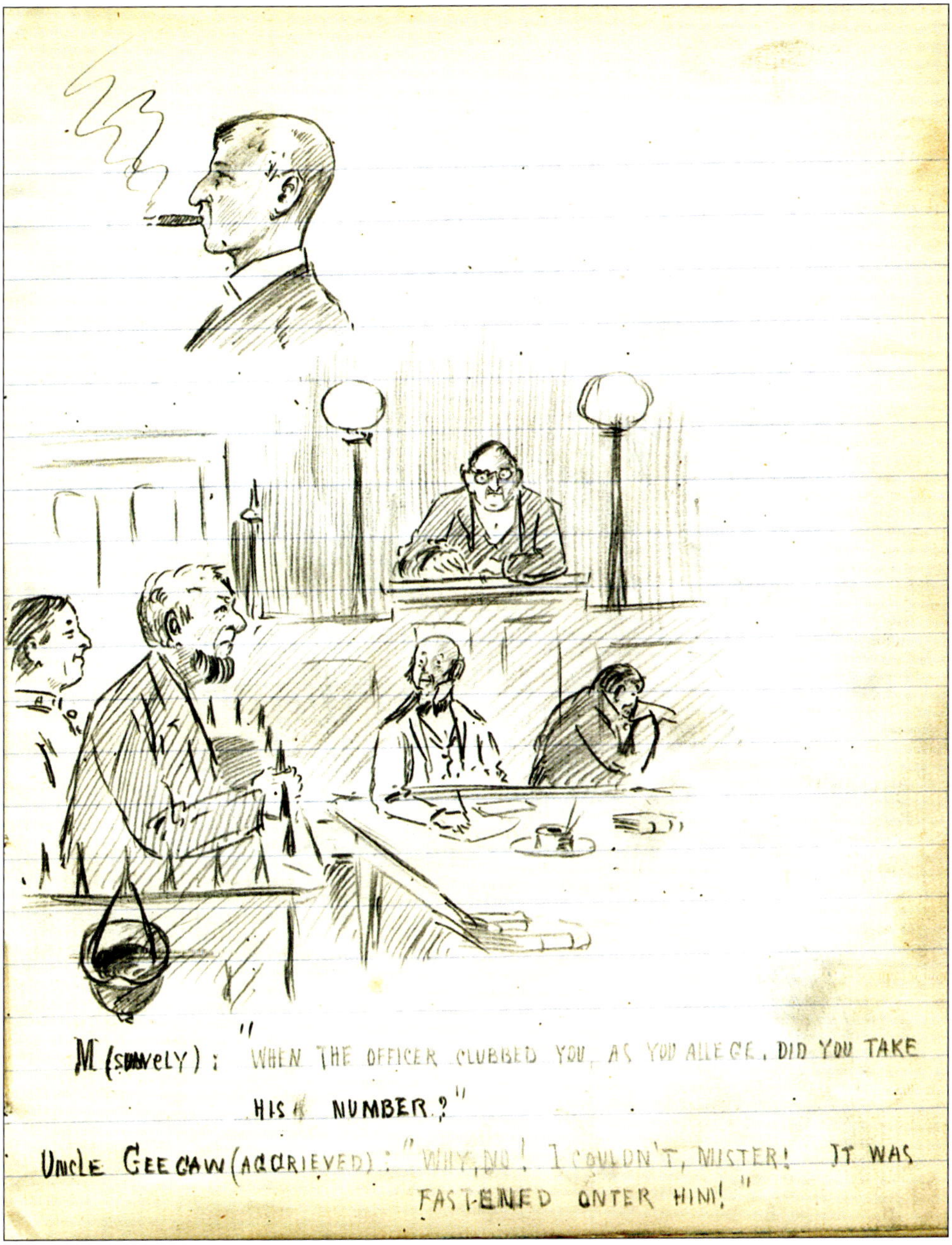

The accumulation of various individual character sketches and a caption:
M (severely): "When the officer clubbed you as you allege, did you take his number?"
Uncle Gee Gaw (Aggrieved): "Why no! I couldn't, mister! It was fastened onter him!"

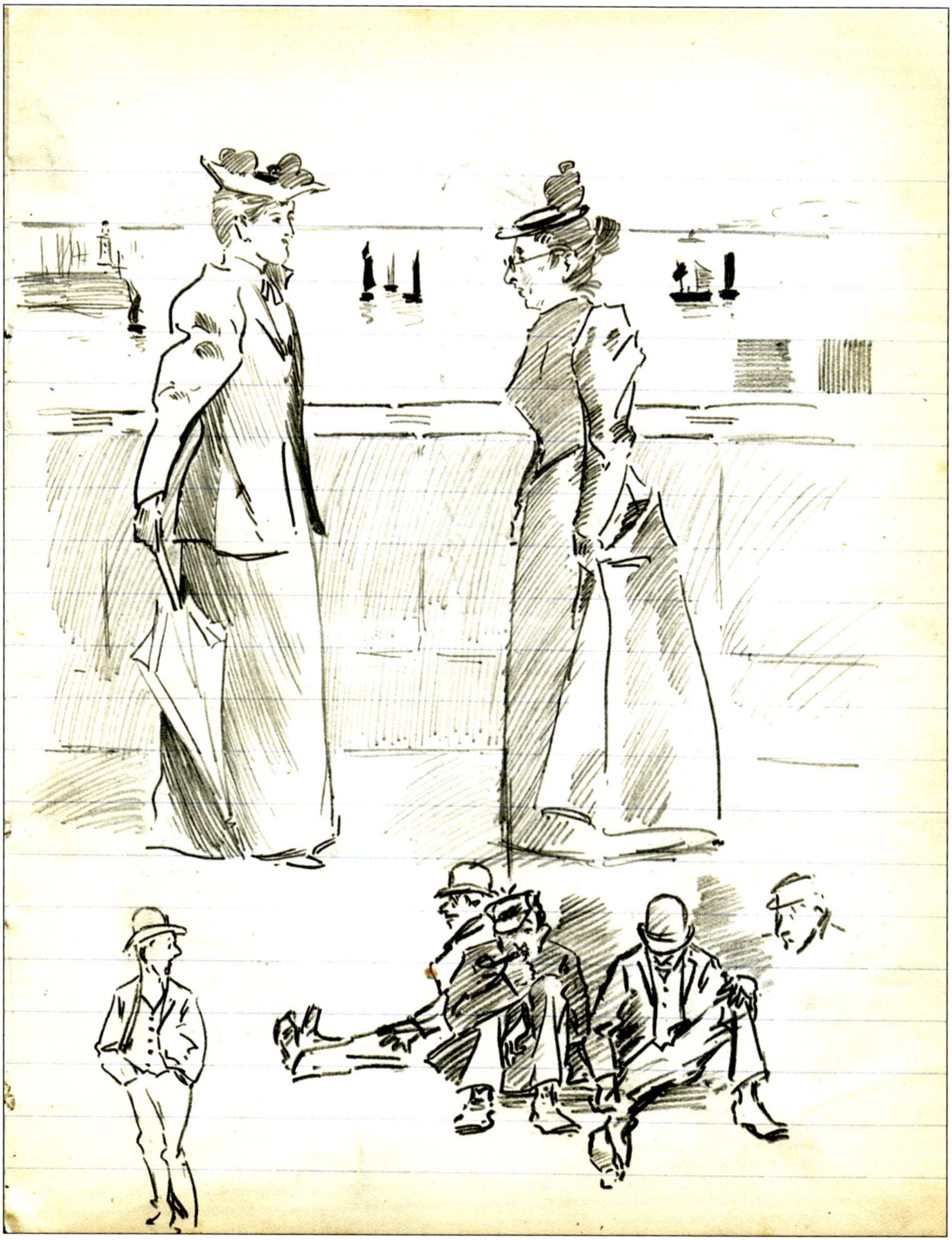

Many of the drawings in the surviving sketch book were of London scenes which would suggest that he travelled to the capital in about 1895. There he took every opportunity to sketch individuals and scenes which would not have been part of his experience in Llangollen.

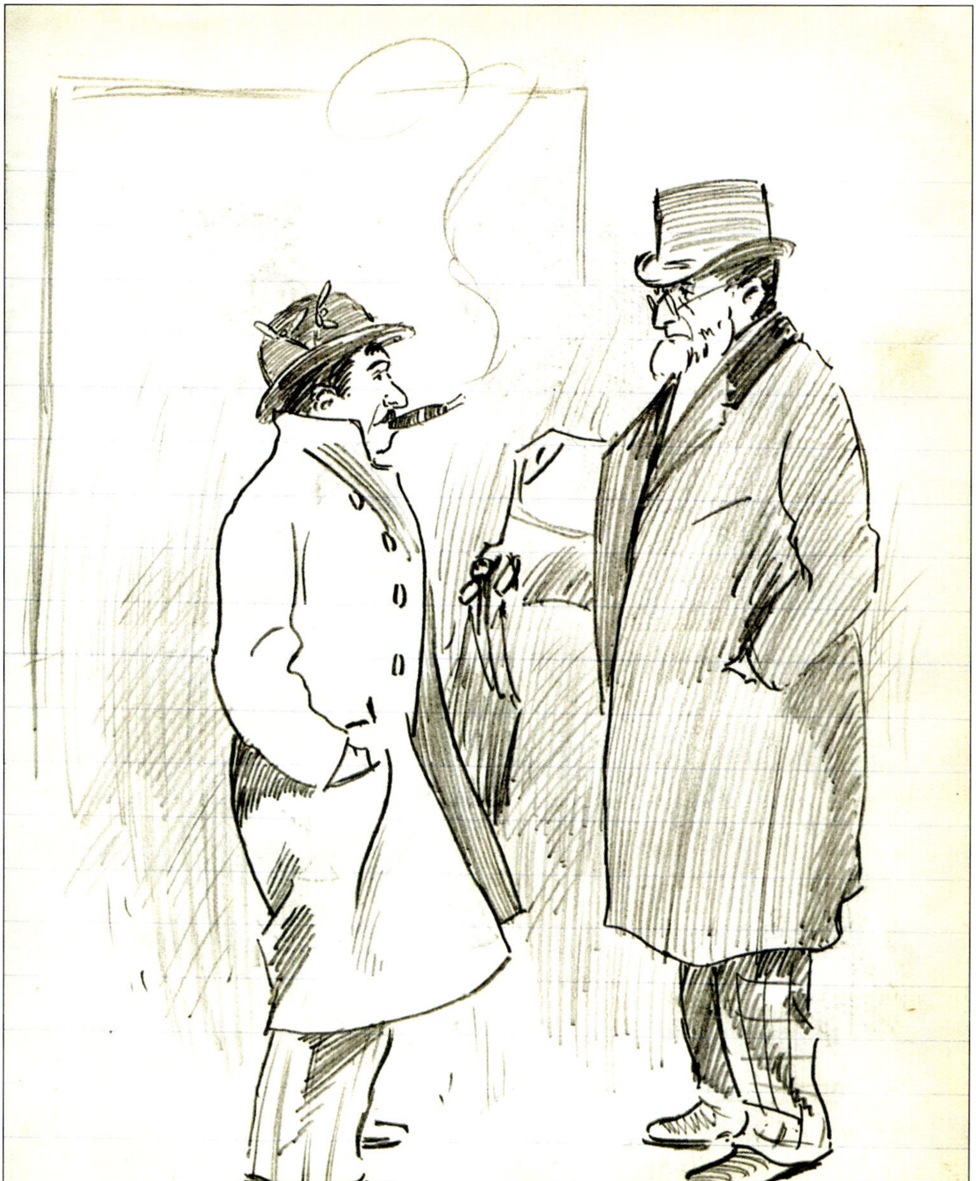

The character in both the faces in this sketch is typical of the numerous studies in the surviving sketch book and clearly illustrates Ernest's natural talent. Here, something of a 'wide boy' (left), smoking a cigar and with some mistletoe tucked into his hat, meets a serious-minded gentleman.

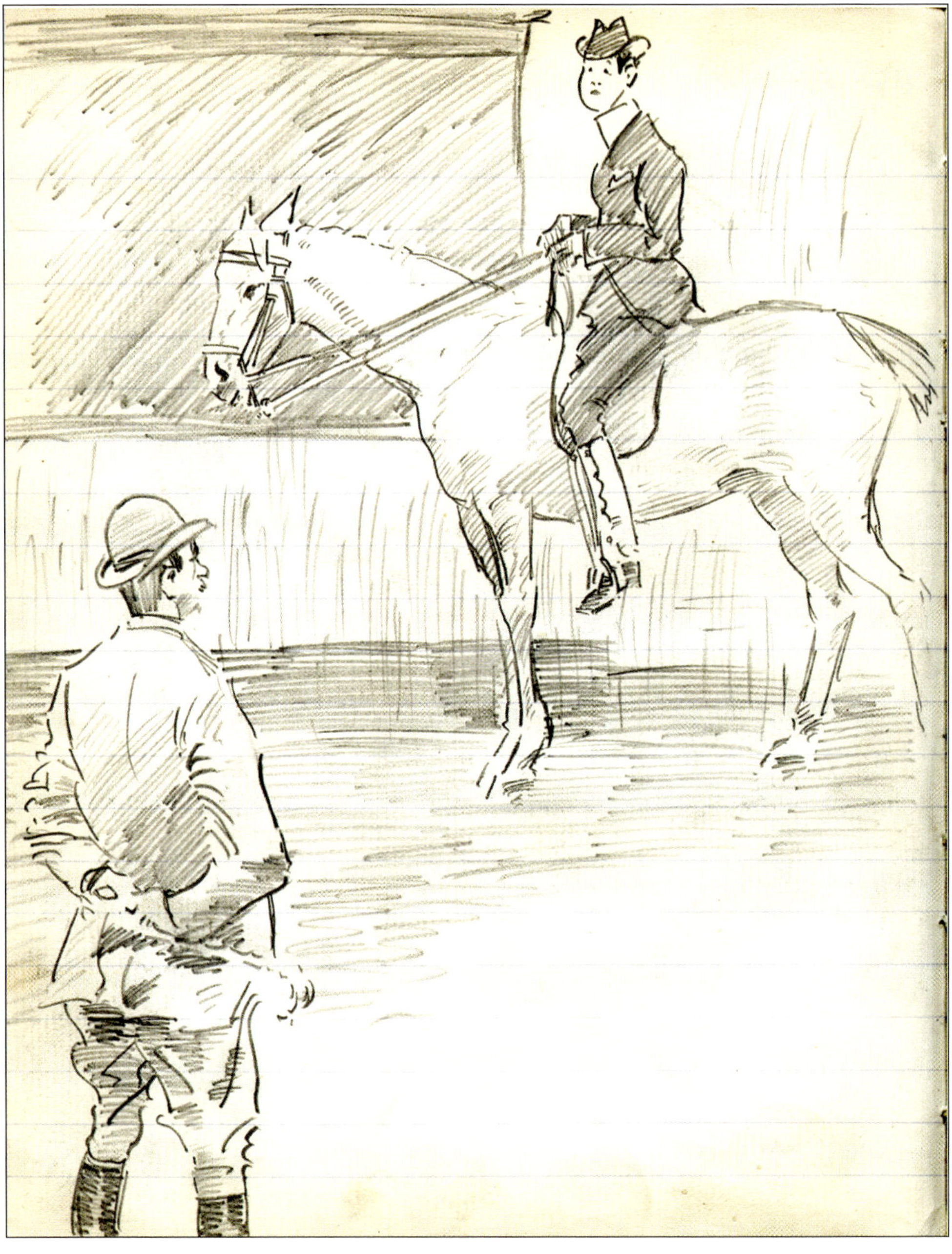

The sketch book contains evidence of his skill at portraying not only people and buildings, but also animals. This simple sketch captures the social class and the worried feel of the rider under instruction from the experienced older man.

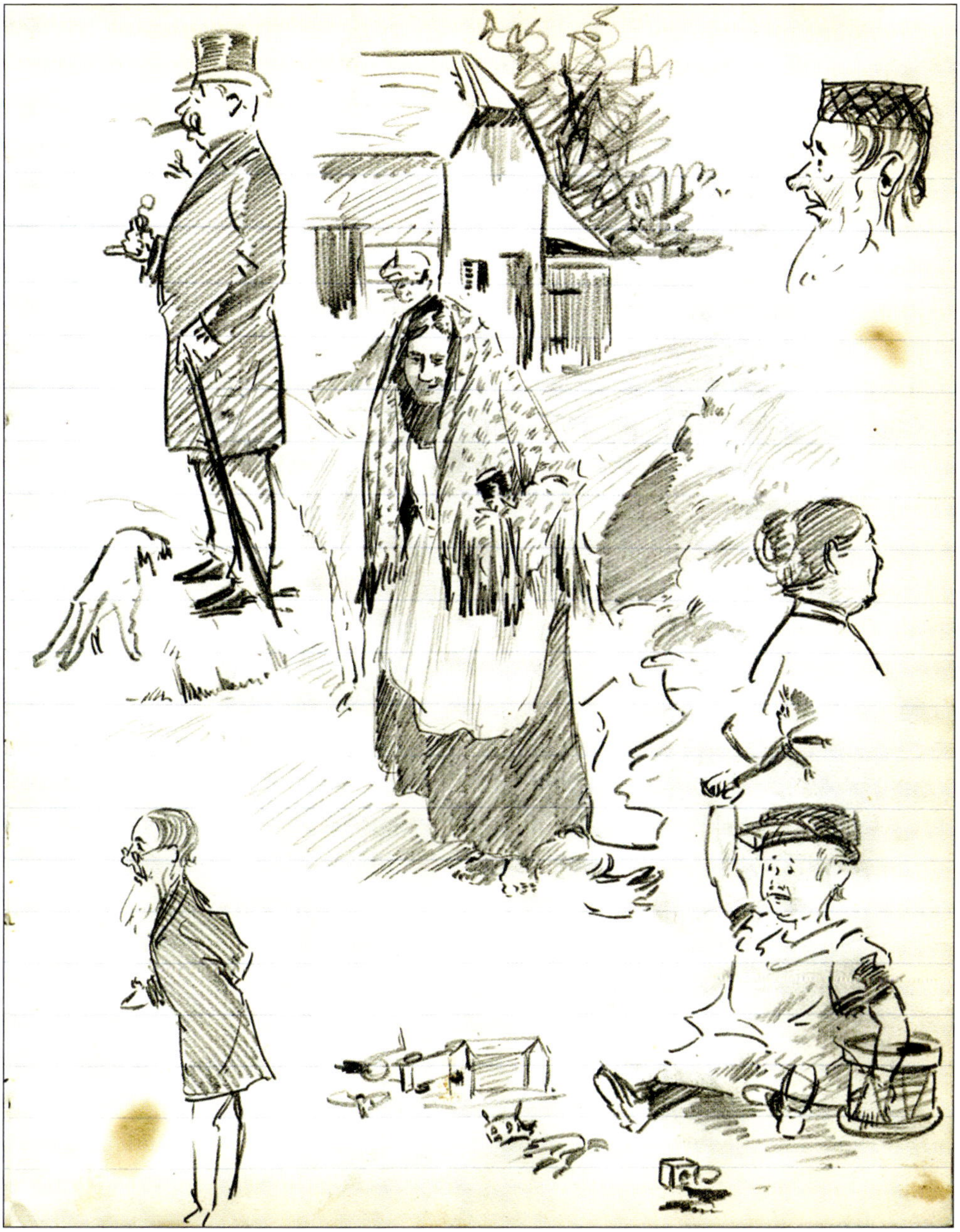

Many of the pages are devoted to numerous character sketches, drawn for possible use at some future date.

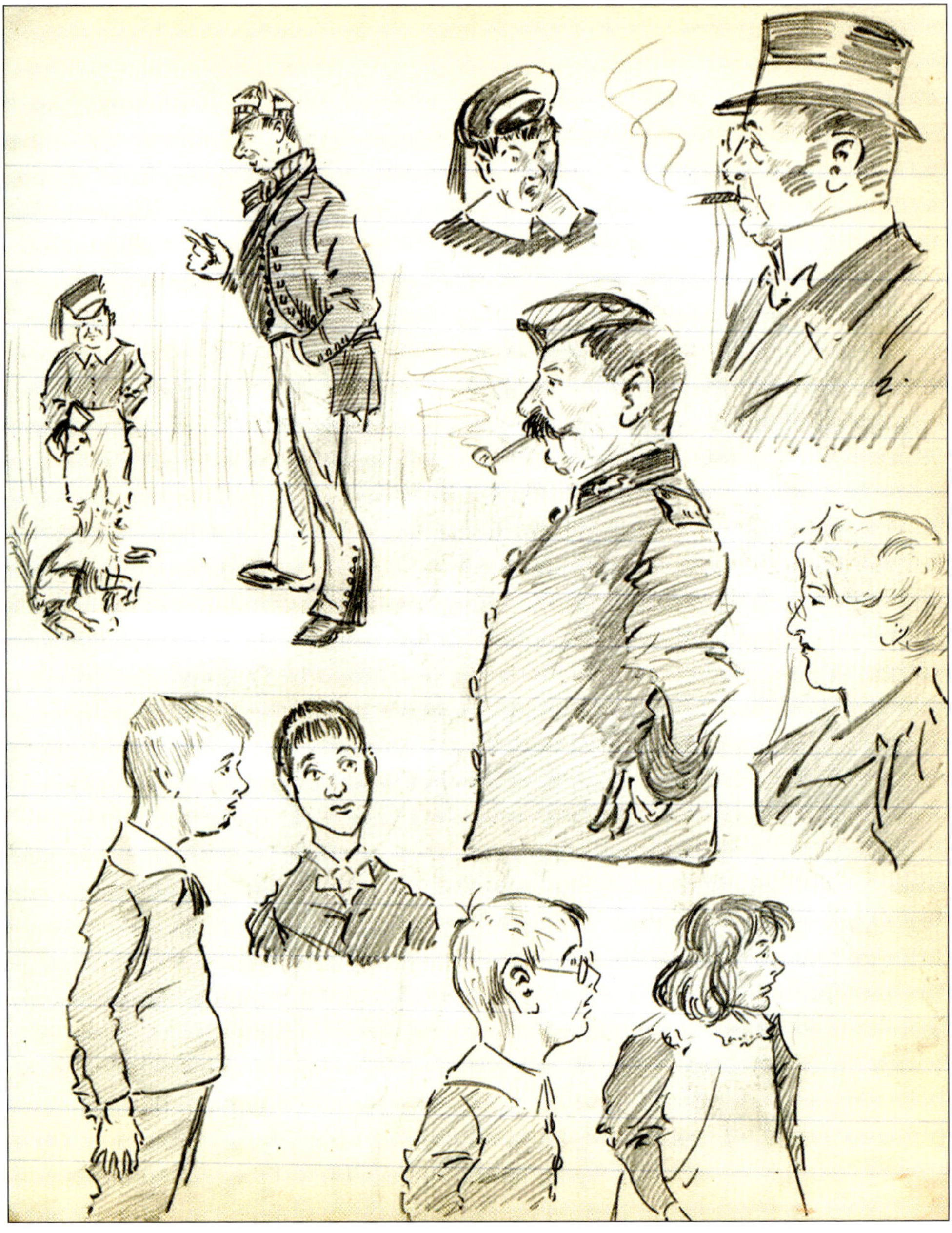

A further selection of character sketches but these could not all have been drawn from life as the fashions depicted (e.g. the three boys top left) are from a period well before the 1890s.